...istory:

...y Short Introduction

VERY SHORT INTRODUCTIONS are for anyone wanting a stimulating and accessible way in to a new subject. They are written by experts and have been translated into more than 40 different languages.

The series began in 1995 and now covers a wide variety of topics in every discipline. The VSI library now contains more than 400 volumes—a Very Short Introduction to everything from Indian philosophy to psychology and American History—and continues to grow in every subject area.

Very Short Introductions available now:

ACCOUNTING Christopher Nobes
ADVERTISING Winston Fletcher
AFRICAN AMERICAN RELIGION
    Eddie S. Glaude Jr.
AFRICAN HISTORY John Parker and
    Richard Rathbone
AFRICAN RELIGIONS Jacob K. Olupona
AGNOSTICISM Robin Le Poidevin
ALEXANDER THE GREAT
    Hugh Bowden
AMERICAN HISTORY Paul S. Boyer
AMERICAN IMMIGRATION
    David A. Gerber
AMERICAN LEGAL HISTORY
    G. Edward White
AMERICAN POLITICAL HISTORY
    Donald T. Critchlow
AMERICAN POLITICAL PARTIES
    AND ELECTIONS
    L. Sandy Maisel
AMERICAN POLITICS Richard M. Valelly
THE AMERICAN PRESIDENCY
    Charles O. Jones
AMERICAN SLAVERY
    Heather Andrea Williams
THE AMERICAN WEST Stephen Aron
ANAESTHESIA Aidan O'Donnell
ANARCHISM Colin Ward
ANCIENT EGYPT Ian Shaw
ANCIENT EGYPTIAN ART AND
    ARCHITECTURE Christina Riggs
ANCIENT GREECE Paul Cartledge
THE ANCIENT NEAR EAST
    Amanda H. Podany
ANCIENT PHILOSOPHY Julia Annas

ANCIENT WARFARE Harry Sidebottom
ANGELS David Albert Jones
ANGLICANISM Mark Chapman
THE ANGLO-SAXON AGE John Blair
THE ANIMAL KINGDOM
    Peter Holland
ANIMAL RIGHTS David DeGrazia
THE ANTARCTIC Klaus Dodds
ANTISEMITISM Steven Beller
ANXIETY
    Daniel Freeman and Jason Freeman
THE APOCRYPHAL GOSPELS
    Paul Foster
ARCHAEOLOGY Paul Bahn
ARCHITECTURE Andrew Ballantyne
ARISTOCRACY William Doyle
ARISTOTLE Jonathan Barnes
ART HISTORY Dana Arnold
ART THEORY Cynthia Freeland
ASTROBIOLOGY David C. Catling
ATHEISM Julian Baggini
AUGUSTINE Henry Chadwick
AUSTRALIA Kenneth Morgan
AUTISM Uta Frith
THE AVANT GARDE David Cottington
THE AZTECS Davíd Carrasco
BACTERIA Sebastian G. B. Amyes
BARTHES Jonathan Culler
THE BEATS David Sterritt
BEAUTY Roger Scruton
BESTSELLERS John Sutherland
THE BIBLE John Riches
BIBLICAL ARCHAEOLOGY
    Eric H. Cline
BIOGRAPHY Hermione Lee

Available soon:

For more information visit our web site

www.oup.com/vsi/

Donald T. Critchlow

AMERICAN POLITICAL HISTORY

A Very Short Introduction

OXFORD
UNIVERSITY PRESS

OXFORD

UNIVERSITY PRESS

Oxford University Press is a department of the
University of Oxford. It furthers the University's objective
of excellence in research, scholarship, and education
by publishing worldwide.

Oxford   New York

Auckland   Cape Town   Dar es Salaam   Hong Kong   Karachi
Kuala Lumpur   Madrid   Melbourne   Mexico City   Nairobi
New Delhi   Shanghai   Taipei   Toronto

With offices in

Argentina   Austria   Brazil   Chile   Czech Republic   France   Greece
Guatemala   Hungary   Italy   Japan   Poland   Portugal   Singapore
South Korea   Switzerland   Thailand   Turkey   Ukraine   Vietnam

Oxford is a registered trade mark of Oxford University Press
in the UK and certain other countries.

Published in the United States of America by
Oxford University Press
198 Madison Avenue, New York, NY 10016

© Oxford University Press 2015

Library of Congress Cataloging-in-Publication Data
Critchlow, Donald T., 1948–
American political history : a very short introduction / Donald T. Critchlow.
pages   cm
Includes bibliographical references and index.
ISBN 978-0-19-934005-7 (acid-free paper)
1. United States—Politics and government.
2. Political culture—United States—History.   I. Title.
E183.C875   2015
320.0973—dc23   2014028718

Printed by Integrated Books International, United States of America
on acid-free paper

To Charles Sellers and Samuel Haber,
my Berkeley mentors

Contents

American Political History

List of illustrations

Acknowledgments

The author appreciates the close reading of many drafts of this book by William Rorabaugh, Lisa Forshaw, Calvin Schermerhorn, Catherine O'Donnell, Gregory Schneider, and Patricia Powers. The two anonymous readers for this manuscript made valuable recommendations for revision. In addition I want to thank Nancy Toff and Rebecca Hecht at Oxford University Press for their editorial assistance.

Introduction

The Founding Fathers who drafted the U.S. Constitution in 1787 feared political parties, popular democracy, and centralized government. Contrary to these sentiments, the national politics that emerged has been that of intense partisan conflict, the continual expansion of suffrage, and the expansion of federal power. Early on, American politics became a blood sport with political candidates and officeholders assailing opponents in negative, and often, vicious ways, to win votes within an electorate that had increased in size and expressed a multitude of interests. By the 1830s all politicians, whatever their party affiliation, proclaimed themselves democrats and "men of the people." The only consistency between the Founders' dream for the new republic and what emerged was a profound faith in constitutional government.

This very short introduction explores how national politics changed from what was conceived in 1787 and what followed. Four major themes emerge in this brief study of American political history: the intensity and continuity of partisanship and polarization; the steady expansion of the electorate to be more inclusive; the continuation of debates over the role and power of the federal government; and the importance of the Constitution in framing political debate.

Political parties emerged early in George Washington's first administration, much to his disgust and despair. Thomas Jefferson and James Madison organized the first political party, the Democratic-Republican Party. In response, Alexander Hamilton and John Adams orchestrated the formation of the Federalist Party. These were not well organized on the national level at first, but operated through state and local leaders. Parties appealed to voters—white males—through reason and passion. They purchased newspapers to carry their partisan message to voters.

With the collapse of New England's sectionally based Federalist Party following the War of 1812, American politics experienced a brief calm, the "Era of Good Feelings." The emergence of Jacksonian Democracy in the late 1820s led to the creation of the Whig Party, and with its collapse in the 1850s, the Republican Party formed. Only in the late nineteenth century was a two-party system composed of the Democratic and Republican parties well developed. Even as the two-party system was being established, a dizzying array of other parties formed—the Know-Nothing Party, the Greenback Party, and People's Party, among others. Third-party movements continued into the twentieth century with the Progressive Party, the Socialist Party, the Reform Party, and the Libertarian Party. Nonetheless, antiparty sentiment remained a powerful expression in American politics. The general American public was wary of partisanship, remaining both disgusted and fascinated by politics as a blood sport.

The development of political parties coincided with the expansion of the electorate. Restrictions on voting rights based on property qualifications for white males were eliminated by the 1830s in most states. Black males were granted voting rights following the Civil War, although measures were instituted in Southern states to prevent full black participation. In the early twentieth century women were granted the right to vote, and in the mid-twentieth century, legislation was passed to ensure voting rights to blacks.

The expansion of suffrage came through social movements and political struggle.

The expansion of the electorate changed the tone of American politics. Candidates running for office proclaimed themselves as representing the average American, rallying against elites and elitism. Campaigns against "politics as usual," bossism, backroom politics, and Washington, D.C., became common themes.

The expansion of the electorate also meant that political parties had to put together uneasy coalitions of constituent interests. Regional, economic, racial, ethnic, and gender groups had to be calibrated carefully by parties and candidates. Shifting alliances meant candidates needed to remain flexible if they were to win office. Challengers tapped into new constituencies to defeat incumbents and overturn party leaders.

In the course of these developments, political campaigns became increasingly expensive. The development of television following the Second World War made running presidential campaigns (as well as congressional campaigns) highly expensive. For political candidates it meant a greater reliance on organized special interests and wealthy donors. It also meant that candidates needed to sell themselves to the public through well-conceived, well-orchestrated, and expensive media campaigns. Image became nearly as important as substance in this new media age.

Above all, the Founders feared power, the domination of some men over others. Power in itself was a natural aspect of government and could only be made legitimate through a compact of mutual consent. If left unconstrained, governmental power, they believed, degenerated into tyranny, oligarchy, or mob rule. Power needed to be distributed among the components of society so that no one group could dominate the others and strip others of their rights. Therefore the Founders sought to create balance through the legislative, judiciary, and executive branches of a national government operating in a federal system. States were to function, in effect, as laboratories in democracy.

They envisioned the new federal government as serving as a referee in adjudicating the various sectional, economic, and social interests of the nation. The coercive powers of government were to remain relatively weak, although necessary to national trade, territorial expansion, immigration, relations with Indians, and diplomatic relations with other countries. Government on the federal, state, and local levels was to foster economic development through the chartering and subsidizing of private companies, while ensuring that the rule of law was maintained.

This tension between the adjudicatory and coercive powers of government appeared early in the nation's history when Alexander Hamilton proposed the creation of a centralized bank, high tariffs, and internal taxes. His opponents, Thomas Jefferson and James Madison, viewed Hamilton's plan as a threat to liberty by expanding the coercive powers of government. Debates over the proper role of the federal government intensified in antebellum America over the removal of Indians west of the Mississippi, banking, tariffs, states' rights, and most importantly, slavery. Often the lines of argument became blurred. For example, southern slaveholders argued for states' rights, while insisting that the federal government return escaped slaves in northern states to their owners in the South.

Industrialization, the emergence of national and transnational corporations, a national market, conservation of natural resources, labor conflict, urbanization, and other social problems led reformers and much of the general public to demand the expansion of federal powers. This entailed extending the powers of government to regulate corporations, protect consumers, conserve natural resources, and protect labor rights. Further expansion of federal power came during the 1930s with the creation of the modern welfare state through the establishment of Social Security, unemployment insurance, and workmen's compensation insurance. The Second World War and the Cold War subsequently imparted an even greater role to the federal government. Civil rights activists called for federal involvement in state affairs to end racial segregation and protect the civil rights of blacks. The result was the growth of the size of government and its role in the economy. Those who supported the expansion of the federal government and the extension of the coercive powers of the state, considered them proper and necessary to maintain freedom and ensure the equal rights of all citizens.

The growth of the federal government in the twentieth century became a central topic in modern American politics. Partisan debate over the proper role, size, and nature of government as well as federal waste, budget deficits, and the national debt divided political parties and the general electorate. Special interests that benefited from government regulations, welfare expenditures, government contracts, and consumer and environmental protection came under political attack.

While the specifics of policy debates in the twentieth and twenty-first centuries changed, partisan division was by no means new to American political history. Political polarization framed early debates over the national bank, territorial expansion, slavery, federal regulation, military intervention, voting rights, and executive power. What remained consistent throughout, however, was a belief in the constitutional order that was embodied in the Founders' vision.

Here proved to be the most enduring legacy and the greatest achievement of the Founders of the new American nation. The agreement that constitutional principles must be upheld, even though these principles might be interpreted differently, characterized a unique experiment in republican government that has survived for the last two hundred-plus years. Partisan conflict, slavery, a civil war, and two world wars presented many challenges to this constitutional order. Yet throughout this turmoil, regular elections continued to be held, representatives were elected to office, and the government continued to operate.

The Founders understood that constitutional republics were fragile by their very nature. Few had survived. Corruption, demagoguery, war, and economic turmoil led to the subversion of liberty and to tyranny. History was replete with the failure of republics. The Founders, well aware of these failures, held an abiding faith that a constitutional republic remained the best, albeit not perfect, form of government. Americans have shared this vision, a faith that has been contested by others. American democracy faces new challenges in the twenty-first century. An understanding of where we have come from and an understanding of our political history will help us meet these new challenges.

Chapter 1
The politics of the Constitution, 1787–89

The delegates who gathered in Philadelphia in late May 1787 shared a common belief that what they were about to undertake—the drafting of a new constitution for the nation—was of historic importance. Riding on their shoulders rested the future of their country and the destiny of the world. Failure meant chaos and perhaps the return of oppressive, corrupt, and authoritarian government serving the privileged and oppressing the masses. They agreed that good government needed to protect liberty, property, and individual rights, although exactly what these terms meant remained open for debate. Influenced by their deep reading of European Enlightenment philosophy, of British philosophers John Locke and David Hume, French thinkers Montesquieu and Jean-Jacques Rousseau, and classical Greek and Roman authors, the Philadelphia delegates were well versed in republican theory. They were also politicians with wide practical experience since many had served as representatives in colonial assemblies or state legislatures and in Congress following the revolution. In the end, the constitution blended republican theory and political compromise.

Most delegates were privileged—planters, merchants, lawyers, and doctors. Their sense of honor was integral to understanding their roles at the convention and their vision for the new republican government. The central actors at the convention were state leaders: Virginian George Washington, the military hero of the revolution; the brilliant James Madison, also from Virginia; the aged and well respected Benjamin Franklin from Pennsylvania; Scottish-born lawyer James Wilson, also representing Pennsylvania; West Indies–born New York politician and lawyer Alexander Hamilton; Gouverneur Morris, born to wealth and privilege in New York; and the often inebriated and long-winded Luther Martin from Maryland, who spoke vigorously in opposition to the new constitution as it took shape. He was joined in his opposition at times by two Virginians, the irascible planter Edmund Randolph and George Mason, Madison's most effective opponent. Two eminent leaders, John Adams and Thomas Jefferson, were missing because they were respectively ambassadors to Britain and France. Madison kept Jefferson well informed as to the deliberations.

The men at the Philadelphia Convention in 1787 feared the political and economic disorder that had ensued with the Articles of Confederation, which had been established during the American Revolution a decade earlier. They believed that the excesses of state government and majoritarian rule under the Confederation threatened the nation's great experiment in republican self-rule. Disillusioned with the failure of the Articles of Confederation, distrustful of direct democracy and the passions of the mob, fearful of demagogues, and terrified by centralized government that was corrupted easily by self-interested factions, the Philadelphia delegates nonetheless expressed profound optimism that the American Revolution marked the beginnings of a new epoch in human history—the establishment of a large-scale representative republican government worthy of a continent.

Voices of artisans (with a few exceptions), women, and black slaves were excluded. They were thought to lack the independence of mind, as well as literal self-sufficiency, considered essential to republican citizenship. The delegates distrusted popular democracy, yet sought to create a representative republic based on popular sovereignty. Madison and Hamilton made a sharp distinction between popular, direct democracy and republican government. They justified their suspicions of direct democracy by their study of human nature and historical experience. As Hamilton told Washington after the Philadelphia convention, "Man, after all, is but Man." Many debates at the convention boiled down to the meaning of representative government. Delegates struggled to construct a political order that delicately balanced democratic and republican values; centralized authority and states' rights; local and regional interests; and executive, legislative, and judicial powers. These complex concepts involving representation emerged as the prevailing issues within American politics for the next two and half-plus centuries—and remain with us today, debated within the constitutional framework set by the Founders.

For four often stifling months, delegates debated under a pledge not to report on the proceedings to the press, their states, or the public. The secretive nature of the convention led opponents to charge a political conspiracy. During the convention, tempers exploded. The final document—the Constitution of the United States—revealed politics in action. After drafting and voting to approve the Constitution, the majority of delegates agreed that nine of the thirteen states would be needed to ratify the document. They knew that without ratification by the powerful states such as Virginia, Massachusetts, and New York the document would be meaningless. The debates at Philadelphia and the Constitution's eventual ratification present a fascinating story of how the nation was born through politics. The U.S. Constitution became a sacrosanct document for Americans, but it was also an act of compromise.

During and after the Revolution, an egalitarian spirit swept the land, challenging established religious and social authority. In organizing the Revolution, elites, urban artisans, and backwoods farmers all had supported the cause. Elite political leaders encouraged, although at times with trepidation, mob actions.

Thomas Paine's *Common Sense*, a revolutionary pamphlet published in 1776 declaring democracy was common sense, and Jefferson's Declaration of Independence manifested an egalitarian impulse expressed in the American Revolution. After the war, all authority—except that of the people—appeared to come under assault. In New York, gentlemen and women were mocked by the lower sorts for signs of elitism such as wearing powdered wigs and silk stockings. In Philadelphia, rowdy drunken youth gathered on street corners to accost passing citizens. Ministers in once-staid Boston complained about the new generation. Republican simplicity became the custom in dress and manner. King's College became Columbia College, and Boston's major thoroughfare was named Congress Street. Popular democracy itself seemed out of control.

This was most evident in the state legislatures. Many states expanded the right to vote, by loosening property ownership requirements, although most states restricted the vote. The colonial practice of dividing power among independent executive, legislative, and judicial branches continued, while severely limiting executive power. Unlike appointed colonial royal governors, the new state governors had only limited vetoes, which the legislatures could override. Legislative branches were made more powerful. The state of Pennsylvania, having one of the most radical state constitutions, limited executive power even more by providing for a plural executive council and a unicameral legislature. Many state legislatures enacted measures for debtor relief and issued paper money to alleviate state and personal debt. Such measures heightened merchants' anxieties amid runaway inflation.

Convention delegates believed generally that the Articles of Confederation had failed. Uninstructed by their legislatures, they quickly decided to draft a new national constitution. The only major accomplishment of the Confederation, other than winning the war, was the enactment of land ordinances for western territories. The Land Ordinance of 1785 provided for surveying of federal lands into townships west of the Appalachian Mountains and north of the Ohio River. The Northwest Ordinance of 1787 called for territorial governments in this area, which eventually became the states of Ohio, Indiana, Illinois, Michigan, and Wisconsin. Slavery was prohibited in the territories. The ordinance prevented the United States from establishing its own colonies by creating a pathway to statehood.

During the Revolution, the states created a weak central government through the Articles of Confederation. The national government consisted of little more than a Congress appointed by the state legislatures. The executive branch was virtually nonexistent. There was no judiciary. Each of the thirteen states had one vote in Congress, and important laws required the consent of nine states. Lacking the power to tax, the government was left to beg for money from the states. The Confederation lacked control of interstate commerce, which allowed states to impose tariffs. Articles could be amended only with the consent of all thirteen sovereign states. The result was political deadlock.

Meanwhile, the young nation confronted massive public debt, economic depression, high unemployment, and worthless paper money. State governments such as that for Rhode Island issued new paper money that was mandated as legal tender for all debts inside the state, which outraged merchants having to accept nearly worthless paper. Foreign policy proved equally disastrous. Great Britain encouraged Indians, who had legitimate fears of American expansion, to attack white settlers on the frontier. Spain continued to threaten to close the Mississippi River to American traders by cutting them off from the major port of New Orleans. The outbreak of a rebellion of indebted farmers in western Massachusetts led by Daniel Shays in 1786 sent chills down the spines of established politicians who saw the revolt, incorrectly, as an attack on private property. Hamilton warned "seditions and insurrections are, unhappily, maladies as inseparable from the body politic, as tumors and eruptions from the natural body." If a relatively stable state such as Massachusetts was threatened with rebellion, what state was not vulnerable?

Confronting major domestic and foreign crises, a small group meeting in Annapolis, Maryland, in 1787 accepted Alexander Hamilton's call for a general convention to address these problems. In response, twelve state legislatures sent fifty-five delegates to meet at a convention in Philadelphia that year. Rhode Island, concerned that a rum tax might be imposed, refused to send representatives.

James Madison—a brilliant Virginia lawyer, slaveholder, planter, and politician—expressed particular concern that government was not working under the Articles of Confederation. Before the Philadelphia Convention, which he had played a singularly important role in organizing, Madison took it upon himself to write a draft of a new constitution that became the point of discussion at the convention. He was convinced that a new form of republican government needed to be created to mitigate what he saw as the excesses of majoritarian misrule in the Confederation and within state legislatures. His disillusionment lay in the failings of state legislators and citizens alike. In drafting the outlines of a new constitution, he sought to protect all interests against majorities. The Madisonian institutional solution fashioned a representative government distanced from direct democracy and delicately balanced among three branches— Congress, the presidency, and the judiciary—and allowed for federal regulation of interstate commerce.

While perhaps differing with Madison on particulars, the delegates accepted his view of what constituted good government. Rooted deeply in classical history and republican thought, they believed that a centralized, coercive government posed the greatest threat to individual liberty, derived from natural law and ancient English tradition. Madison proposed increasing federal power, while creating a government that served as referee to adjudicate sectional, social, and political interests. He proposed that this new federal government be empowered to have coercive powers to defend the nation, regulate interstate trade, levy taxes, and maintain order and the rule of law.

Soft-spoken, short, and genteel in manner, the widely read Madison drew his colleagues' respect at the convention for his understanding of republican principles. Distrustful of popular democracy—a lesson he had learned in his study of past constitutions and governments—he proposed to the Philadelphia convention two legislative houses, the House and the Senate, whose memberships were both based on state population. In his so-called Virginia plan, Congress elected the chief executive, who carried the right of veto, as did the judiciary. Madison's plan thwarted direct democracy, while favoring states like Virginia with large populations.

Delegates from states with small populations such as New Jersey proposed that each state, regardless of population, would continue to have equal representation in both houses. Madison and most of the delegates opposed the New Jersey Plan. When it appeared that delegates from the small states were going to walk out and refuse to sign the final draft of the Constitution, they reached a compromise that provided states with equal representation in the Senate and proportional representation based on population in the House. In these last hectic days of the convention, details were worked out on the nature of the executive and judicial branches.

The compromise over representation showed practical politics at work. Yet the final Constitution was not all a matter of pragmatism. Madison and the southern delegates expressed concern early on about protecting slaveholders' rights. Regional distinctions between nonslaveholding and slaveholding states, Madison and southern delegates argued, were real. They feared that commercial and maritime states such as Pennsylvania might subordinate landed interests of the South and the West. Southern states demanded that slaves be counted for apportioning representation, based on population in the House. This was a matter of principle. Northern delegates finally accepted an accommodation with slavery as a price of union. As a plum to the South, slaves were counted as three-fifths of their total number, thereby ensuring larger slaveholder representation in the House. The three-fifths compromise was based on a 1783 amendment in the Articles of Confederation for apportioning state taxes. In another compromise, in late August the convention agreed that Congress could not prohibit the importation of slaves prior to 1808. (After 1808 Congress would ban the importation of slaves.)

The delegates decided that the Constitution needed to be ratified by nine of the thirteen states through conventions called by the legislatures. The erudite Gouverneur Morris put the final touches on the document, organizing sections and polishing language, including the striking preamble, "We the people in order to form a more perfect union..." On September 17 the convention adjourned for the last time. The fight for ratification began one of the most vigorous political campaigns in American history.

Proponents of the proposed Constitution cleverly labeled themselves Federalists, leaving opponents as the Anti-Federalists. Both sides agreed that the Constitution needed to be ratified through the popular sovereignty of the citizens. Rhetoric during the Revolution and its aftermath proclaimed the people as the source of political legitimacy, but who "the people" actually were remained vague. Neither side placed much confidence in the people because they feared cunning leaders easily manipulated them, although Anti-Federalists often spoke the language of popular democracy. The debate came down to whether the new Constitution fulfilled the promise of the American Revolution or repudiated it.

The battle over ratification was waged through polemical pamphlets, newspapers, and rallies, all calculated to influence voters in picking delegates to the states' ratifying conventions. Voter qualifications were determined by each state and varied considerably. A majority of white men could vote in most states, but property qualifications were high in a few. Property-owning women could vote in New Jersey. Free blacks could vote in some states. Slaves were considered property and could not vote. Urban artisans and small shopkeepers rallied behind the new Constitution. Wealthy merchants and planter aristocrats were divided, as were backcountry farmers. They wanted protection from Indian attacks but feared coercive authority. Regional icons such as Virginia's Patrick Henry and Boston's Samuel Adams emerged as leading opponents.

Federalists adapted strategies appropriate to the political circumstances of each state. George Washington, who enjoyed universal popularity, imparted prestige to the Federalist cause. Federalists exerted intellectual firepower when Madison, Hamilton, and John Jay, a persuasive New York lawyer, joined forces to write eighty-five brilliant newspaper articles—later known as the Federalist Papers—to defend and explain the new Constitution. Hamilton wrote the bulk of the essays, fifty-one, while Madison authored twenty-six of the essays that appeared between September 1787 and August 1788. Throughout most states, the press favored the Federalist cause, and opponents were on the defensive in most states.

Anti-Federalists rallied around a strategy of insisting upon the adoption of amendments including a Bill of Rights to protect individual rights. Although they differed on many specifics, they feared that the Constitution granted to the federal government too much coercive power. They accepted, however, that the Philadelphia convention had the authority to draft a new Constitution, but they opposed the final product. Anti-Federalists failed to offer a collective critique of the new Constitution. Many expressed general sentiment that the Philadelphia convention was a conspiratorial cabal of powerful men who distrusted popular democracy. Anti-Federalists drew support from northern and western New England, Rhode Island, New York's Hudson Valley, western Pennsylvania, southern Virginia, North Carolina, and upcountry South Carolina. They drew from the same tradition as the Federalists: civic republicanism, Protestantism, and the traditions of English common law. The fundamental difference separating the two sides was Anti-Federalist fears of centralized government. They honed in on the omission of a bill of rights, consolidation of power, charges of aristocratic government, threats of high taxation, and fears about the creation of a standing army.

Anti-Federalist Arthur Lee expressed the common belief of opponents to the Constitution when he warned that ratification meant the destruction of "the liberties of the people." Echoing this anxiety, another Anti-Federalist declared, "When a tyranny is established, there are always masters as well as slaves." Class-conscious rhetoric found common expression in Anti-Federalist tracts, even though the spokesmen came from the upper and middling classes.

Ratification gained easy victories in early state conventions. Even in Pennsylvania, where the Anti-Federalists were well organized, ratification carried by two to one. Although New Hampshire became the crucial ninth state to ratify, two key states remained outside. In the battleground state of Virginia, federalists achieved ratification in a contentious vote. After Virginia's decision, New York, led by Hamilton and New York City delegates, barely achieved ratification by three votes. In Langsingburgh and Halfmoon, New York, women paraded in honor of New York's ratification. In more destructive fashion, a pro-Federalist mob broke into the press of the Anti-Federalist *New York Journal*, destroying its type. With New York ratification in hand, North Carolina followed with its approval. Obstinate Rhode Island grudgingly approved ratification in 1790, after the new federal government had been established. George Washington won easy and uncontested election to the presidency.

1. President George Washington stands before Congress delivering his first inaugural speech in 1789. As the nation's commander in chief, he holds a military sword, while his other hand rests on the Constitution. A young boy, representing the future of the nation, stands before him.

The battle over ratification left hard feelings. When elections to the First Congress were held a short time later, candidates' original stance on ratification proved important. The new Senate had two vocal Anti-Federalists, and the House elected fourteen. During the ratification battle, state conventions proposed a total of 124 amendments to the Constitution. One of the first actions of the new Congress was enactment of a "Bill of Rights," consisting of ten amendments to the Constitution, which Madison originally had opposed. The Bill of Rights represented a victory for the Anti-Federalists, who feared that government could not be trusted to stay within the bounds of the Constitution.

Ratification had been won, but the task of establishing a new federal government for the new nation lay ahead.

Chapter 2
Contentious people and factious parties in the Early Republic, 1789–1824

The Founding Fathers feared political factions as a natural corruption of democrat government. None envisioned the rise of the severe factionalism that arose during Washington's administration from 1789 to 1797. Divisions occurred over Secretary of the Treasury Alexander Hamilton's plans for the federal government to assume states' debts, establish a national bank, raise taxes, and pursue a pro-British foreign policy. Secretary of State Thomas Jefferson and James Madison, believing Hamilton's proposals were unconstitutional, vehemently opposed the Hamiltonian program. Thought officially neutral, President Washington always seemed to side with Hamilton. At the root of this factionalism were opposing visions for the future of the nation. Opponents of Hamilton's plans feared the creation of a coercive centralized government that served financial and political special interests.

These competing visions gave rise to quasi-political parties, the Democrats and the Federalists. Both sides claimed to represent democratic principles and invectively attacked their opponents for betraying the Constitution. Jeffersonian Democrats (initially known as the Democratic-Republican party) proved more effective in rallying average voters. Ultimately the largely New England-based Federalist party collapsed during the War of 1812. This period saw the first signs of partisan politics appealing to the common man, even though suffrage remained restricted.

By the time a disgusted Washington left office in 1797, clear factions within the country had emerged: Federalists aligned with Hamilton's program and Democrats who supported Jefferson's and Madison's call for a strict interpretation of the Constitution, a small federal government, and states' rights. Federalists responded by arguing that the establishment of a central bank, protective tariffs, and the assumption of state debts served the larger national interests within the intent of the framers of the Constitution. At a time when the word "party" was almost a swear word, both factions denied they were forming parties and in fact publicly denounced parties as a threat to the republic. Hamilton warned that factions were "the natural disease of popular governments."

Accusations of conspiracies ran rampant on both sides, with Federalists denouncing their opponents as pro-French radical egalitarian Jacobins, while Jeffersonians remained convinced that Hamilton and his allies sought to create a an urbanized, centralized nation. In this vituperative, highly charged atmosphere, in which parties had only rudimentary existence, gossip and broadsides proliferated and public demonstrations turned violent, both Hamiltonians and Jeffersonians nonetheless saw themselves as "men of honor" following ritualized codes of behavior. Within this code of honor, politicians denounced political parties and self-gain in favor of democratic virtue, high principle, and elite leadership.

Having been elected unanimously and without contest by the first Electoral College, George Washington entered the presidency intent on setting a high moral tone and establishing precedents embodying democratic principles. To provide geographic balance, John Adams of Massachusetts was elected vice president. Washington's cabinet included Hamilton to spearhead Treasury and John Jay at the Department of State, later replaced by Thomas Jefferson.

Washington's administration quickly became mired in factional dispute. At stake between Hamilton and Jefferson-Madison were perspectives of the country's future. Jefferson articulated his goal for the new nation in *Notes on the State of Virginia* (1787), in which he championed rural life. For him, the backbone of any republic rested in an independent, small-scale, landholding yeomanry. He viewed cities as generators of disease, poverty, and corruption. Urban wage labor, he believed, sapped the manly independence of citizens. His beliefs were deeply rooted in his wide reading of ancient history and eighteenth-century liberal political thought, an abiding faith in "the people," and his experience of living in squalid London and Paris. Jefferson distrusted large-scale manufacturing and advocated small-household manufacturing. Future population growth meant that westward expansion remained essential to his vision of agrarian democracy. At the same time he was a large slaveholding planter, increasingly insistent in his later years on slaveholders' rights.

Hamilton proposed that the federal government develop industries and commercial trade. His *Report on Manufacturers* (1791), written at the request of Washington, called for protective tariffs (i.e., taxes on imports) and a national bank to aid domestic commercial development, create a prosperous urban artisan workforce, and promote a self-sufficient economy. Ideology as well as personal rivalry divided Jefferson and Hamilton.

The first major issue confronted by the new government was what to do with old war debts and the worthless paper money that was still circulating. Secretary of the Treasury Hamilton, a believer in a strong national government, proposed that the federal government fund Confederation debts by repurchasing bonds at face value, even though the market value of these bonds had fallen dramatically. Hamilton believed his plan would strengthen the nation's credit. The plan drew immediate criticism from James Madison, floor leader in the House of Representatives. Madison charged that the current holders of the debt were speculators who had bought the Confederation bonds from patriotic, debt-ridden patriots who had sold their nearly worthless bonds at little more than two cents on the dollar. Congress rejected Madison's proposal to pay original bondholders at the original face value and pay later speculators the depreciated market value of the bonds.

Madison was even more outraged over Hamilton's proposal to assume state debts. Southern states, including Madison's home state of Virginia, had paid off their debts. Madison charged that southern states were now being called upon to pay higher taxes to help pay northern states' debts. After Jefferson arranged a dinner meeting between the two men, Madison agreed to the assumption of state debts at face value in return for moving the nation's capital from New York to the Virginia-Maryland border on the Potomac River. While the new city was being built, the capital moved temporarily from New York City to Philadelphia, where it stayed for the next ten years. Pennsylvanians grumbled that the capital might remain there permanently.

In 1791, Hamilton proposed a federally chartered national bank using a public-private partnership inspired by the Bank of England. Hamilton believed the bank offered hope of rationalizing the nation's currency and augmenting its citizens' access to credit. He maintained the bank was constitutional under the commerce clause. Jefferson disagreed, declaring the proposal unconstitutional because it extended power beyond what the framers meant by the "proper and necessary" clause. Washington sided with Hamilton, and the measure passed Congress by a narrow vote.

The chasm between political factions within the administration widened farther when Hamilton proposed a large tax on whiskey distillers in order to increase government revenue. Hamilton's proposal hurt small whiskey distillers relative to rum importers and large domestic whiskey distillers who could afford the tax. In backcountry western Pennsylvania and Kentucky, many farmers drew most of their income from small distilleries. After the Whiskey Tax passed Congress in 1791, Hamilton sent internal revenue agents throughout the country to collect the taxes. Jefferson believed Hamilton was creating a personal political machine of Treasury agents to do his bidding.

Washington easily won reelection in 1792, but the Hamilton-Jefferson feud continued, and Washington grew closer to Hamilton. The feud became entangled in foreign affairs, specifically American relations with warring Britain and France. America engaged in trade with both countries, but they refused to recognize American neutrality. When revolution first broke out in France in 1789, Americans greeted the event with excitement, believing it to be another sign of the new age of democracy. But the French revolution turned more violent with the execution of King Louis XVI, Hamilton and his allies, including many New England Protestant clergymen, reacted in horror. This was not democracy but mob tyranny. When war erupted between France and Britain, Hamilton, an Anglophile, urged a closer relationship with Britain. Jefferson, a Francophile, opposed a pro-British American foreign policy. In 1793 when Washington proclaimed American neutrality in the conflict between the two nations, Jefferson resigned from the cabinet. He went to work with Madison to develop a political movement aimed at stopping the Hamiltonian program.

Further trouble came with the arrival of Edmond Charles Genêt as French ambassador to the United States in April 1793. Citizen Genêt mistook his initially warm reception as a sign of enthusiastic support for the French revolution. Democratic-Republican societies displaying support for France had sprung up throughout the country, largely among urban artisans. Jefferson and Madison kept their distance from this movement with its often belligerent egalitarianism and radicalism. In street demonstrations, Hamilton and other Federalist leaders were burned in effigy. While attracting artisans, the clubs' membership was heterogeneous, including lawyers, merchants, and teachers. What held the clubs together was radical egalitarianism. Some members of the Democratic-Republican Clubs wore red liberty caps in solidarity with the French revolutionaries, and they organized committees of correspondence across state lines. Federalists saw a conspiracy afoot.

Genêt poured fuel on the fire by threatening to go over Washington's head and appealing to the American people to allow the outfitting of private gunships to attack British ships. This was a clear violation of Washington's policy of neutrality. Genêt's ploy backfired when he was perceived as insulting Washington, the hero of the American Revolution. Federalists unleashed a barrage of public and private attacks on Genêt trying to link him with Jefferson and Madison. Under political attack, the two Virginians sought to distance themselves from the French ambassador. Finally, Washington ordered the irascible man back to France, but Genêt's enemies came to power in France, and he remained in the United States as a political refugee.

The Genêt affair placed Jefferson on the defensive, but protests on the frontier over the whiskey tax caused resentment toward Hamilton's program. In 1794, farmers in western Pennsylvania rebelled against tax collectors. In July the rebellion turned violent when 500 armed men attacked the home of the unpopular federal excise inspector, ransacking and burning the property to the ground. Insurgents spoke of attacking Pittsburgh. An alarmed Hamilton persuaded Washington that this was an insurrection, and 13,000 militia, mostly from Virginia, were called out to suppress the insurgency. Twenty of the whiskey rebels were arrested, although all were later acquitted or pardoned.

Domestic turmoil encouraged Washington to seek conciliation abroad. He sent John Jay to England as a special envoy to convince Britain to recognize American neutrality and to stop impressing American seamen into the British navy. This British practice of seizing American sailors (who did not carry citizenship papers) from U.S. vessels on the high seas outraged Americans.

Jay, anxious to ease tensions, agreed to what essentially was a treaty that did not recognize American neutrality rights or stop impressment. Jeffersonians denounced Jay's Treaty publicly and in the halls of Congress. The Jay Treaty divided the nation as never before. After a furious debate, the Senate reluctantly approved the treaty in 1795.

George Washington expressed growing disillusionment with politics. He enjoyed some success in signing the Treaty of Greenville with twelve Indian tribes, following the defeat of a loose confederation of tribes at Fallen Timbers in Ohio the previous year. The treaty ceded much of the area to white settlement. In late 1795, Washington scored another triumph with Pinckney's Treaty with Spain, which confirmed United States' southern boundary with Spanish Florida and gave American farmers the right to ship goods down the Mississippi River to New Orleans, which was controlled by Spain. Washington refused a third term out of respect for democratic principle and because he was fed up with politics. In his farewell address, he lamented the rise of political parties and warned against permanent foreign alliances.

By the time Washington left office in 1797, the Democrat and Federalist factions were well cemented. These distinct factions, however, should not be seen as mass political parties like those we have today. Democrats and Federalists are best described as "proto-parties," organized around political leaders and party newspapers. Because "party" was an odious word in the eighteenth century, leaders of both factions denied they were forming political parties. Both spoke of representing democratic principles that could only be subverted by the formation of political parties. Neither faction believed in the concept of a loyal opposition acting as a rival political party. Political victory meant permanently driving out the other faction.

Both factions viewed themselves as providing elite leadership to the masses. The task of politicians was to represent the people and instruct voters. Jeffersonians spoke the language of democracy more readily than the Federalists and appeared more willing to "court" the voters. In this way, Jeffersonians tapped into a popular democratic political culture that had deepened following the American Revolution.

The 1796 election pitted the two factions against one another in the nation's first contested presidential election. John Adams won with 71 electoral votes; his rival Jefferson received 68 electoral votes, which gave him the vice presidency. In only half of the sixteen states did voters directly choose presidential electors, while legislatures in other states appointed electors. This election showed that a crude two-party system had emerged, with electioneering, organizing, and the construction of political tickets.

Adams came into office seeking factional reconciliation, but hopes of political harmony were quickly dashed by a diplomatic crisis and quasi-war with France. When Adams sent a diplomatic mission to France to avoid war, he ruptured relations with anti-French Hamiltonians within the Federalists, and he alienated Jefferson, who believed a Democrat should have been appointed to the commission. At this point Jefferson reached out to Aaron Burr in New York to begin organizing Democrats in that state. When unofficial French representatives—later dubbed X, Y, and Z—tried to extort a bribe from the American delegation, Americans became outraged by this insult. Anti-French feelings swept across America, placing Jeffersonians once again on the defensive.

At this point, the Federalists overplayed their hand by seeking legislation to crush the opposition. In the summer of 1798, Federalists passed three repressive antialien acts and an ominous Sedition Law that made it unlawful to impede the operation of any law or intimidate any person holding public office. The acts created martyrs for the Democrats to rally around when a number of editors such as William Duane, editor of the *Philadelphia*

Aurora, were arrested for sedition. At the same time, these acts aggravated sectional tensions in the South.

These sectional tensions manifested themselves in resolutions enacted in Virginia and Kentucky arguing that states could nullify federal laws that were determined to be unconstitutional by state legislatures. Working behind the scenes, a deeply disturbed Vice President Jefferson joined with Madison in secretly drafting these resolutions. They labeled the Alien and Sedition Laws unconstitutional. Jefferson's agent in Virginia, Wilson Cary Nicholas, gave the resolution to a legislator in Kentucky to introduce after being sworn to secrecy to keep the vice president's name out of the controversy. In Virginia, Madison, at Jefferson's insistence, drafted a more radical version of the resolution, stating that a state could declare a federal law null and void. Federalists pointed out that Democrats had been responsible for the Virginia Sedition Act in 1792, which punished slanderous and libelous assertions, but charges of hypocrisy were not an effective argument. The resolutions were intended to defend personal liberty and restrain the coercive powers of the federal government. Two decades later, Southerners employed this doctrine of nullification to defend slavery and states' rights, hardly an expression of a belief in universal personal liberty. The resolutions also show states serving as policy laboratories, in this case to the detriment of federal power.

The Alien and Sedition Acts revealed that Adams's policy of factional reconciliation had failed. At the same time, Adams found himself embattled within his own administration by Hamiltonian Federalists who accused him of moderation and political ineptitude. Federalists entered the 1800 presidential elections badly split, a fissure which had widened when Hamilton tried to prevent Adams's renomination for a second term.

The election of 1800 was the first election without Washington, who died in late 1799. The critical turning point in the election came in May when the returns of the New York legislature came in giving the state to the Democrats. The campaign had been carefully orchestrated by Burr, who organized New York City down to the precinct level and tapped new faces to run for office. Burr's success prompted Jefferson to put him on the ticket as his vice-presidential running mate. The election took place in the states from May to December. In ten of the sixteen states, legislators chose the electors. When the returns were finally tallied, Jefferson and Burr received the identical number of electoral votes, seventy-three, to Adams's sixty-five. The Constitution called for the top vote-getter to be president and the runner-up to be vice president. (Adams would have won the election in all likelihood if the three-fifths clause had not given fourteen electoral votes to the South based on its slave population).

The electoral tie threw the final outcome of the election to the House of Representatives. Had the Democrats been a truly united party, the House would have picked Jefferson, the party's presidential choice, over Burr, the vice-presidential candidate. Instead there was intrigue. Under the Constitution each state was allowed to cast a single vote, which meant in 1800 that nine of the sixteen votes were needed to win. Determined to prevent Jefferson from gaining the White House, some Federalist legislators supported Burr. Fearful of a Burr presidency, Hamilton cajoled Federalists to support Jefferson. (The personal and political antagonism between Burr and Hamilton led to a duel in 1804 in which Hamilton died.) House voting began in February. After thirty ballots the deadlock was broken when Federalist James Bayard from Delaware left town and allowed Delaware's vote to go to Jefferson. Two hostile parties agreed to transfer power peacefully.

Jefferson proclaimed the election the "Revolution of 1800," although it marked a peaceful transfer of power between hostile political parties. This description was correct in the sense that the Virginia dynasty of Jefferson, Madison, and Monroe controlled the White House for the next twenty-four years. In his inaugural address, Jefferson called for the end of partisanship. Despite this reconciliatory tone, Jefferson tried to impeach several Federalist judges. This action failed. In 1803, Chief Justice John Marshall expanded the Supreme Court's power by declaring, in *Marbury v. Madison* (1803), the court had the right to pass on the constitutionality of federal laws.

Jefferson's greatest achievement in his first term was the purchase of the Louisiana territory from France. In 1803, the debt-ridden Napoleon offered to sell the Louisiana territory to the United States at a bargain price. Jefferson undertook this purchase through executive action—a remarkable extension of presidential powers. The landmass of the United States doubled in this single deal. Shortly after the purchase, Jefferson commissioned the Lewis and Clark expedition to explore western lands to the Pacific. Along the way, the expedition offered peace medals to various Indian tribes. Nonetheless, some Indian leaders, such as Tecumseh of the Shawnee confederation, resisted American westward expansion. Jefferson won reelection in 1804 against a faction-ridden, New England-based, Federalist opposition. Democratic-Democrats, as the party now increasingly called itself, won control of both houses of Congress.

America's extension to the west through the Louisiana Purchase fostered Jefferson's dreams of building a white democracy of small-scale subsistence farmers. Not all was tranquil in the west, however. In 1807, former Vice President Aaron Burr was arrested and charged with treason for trying to organize a plot to establish a new western republic in the former Spanish territory of the Mississippi River valley. In the subsequent trial before Chief Justice John Marshall, Burr was acquitted under a strict definition of treason, but his political career was over.

Whatever confidence Jefferson felt about the future of the nation in the west, it failed to allay his frustration with Britain's intransigence about accepting American claims of neutrality in shipping. A less Anglophobic president might have better understood Britain's need to cut American shipping to its enemy Napoleon, but Jefferson was convinced that England could be forced to accommodate U.S. demands because it was reliant on American goods. Finally, an exasperated Jefferson pressured Congress to enact a trade embargo that prohibited American ships from leaving their ports to engage in foreign trade. The Jefferson administration imposed draconian enforcement of this legislation. Unfortunately, the embargo led to severe economic hardship in New England and eventual war with England.

Jefferson's popularity, and the disorganization of the Federalists, enabled him to pass the presidential mantle to his close friend Madison in 1808. Federalists had been reduced to a feckless opposition without much strength outside of New England. A few Democratic-Democrats aligned with Madison's opponent, John Randolph, who tried to rally behind James Monroe, but Jefferson backed Madison. Perhaps if the embargo had become law earlier and its full economic effects felt, Federalist candidate Charles C. Pinckney might have done better in the presidential election. Madison defeated Pinckney 122 to 47 in the Electoral College.

2. This 1801 Jefferson peace medal was carried westward by the Lewis and Clark expedition as a gift of friendship to Native Americans. The two clasping hands indicate that at this time Americans recognized Indian sovereignty, a policy changed by Andrew Jackson three decades later. The other side of the medal depicts Jefferson in profile.

For all of his intellectual brilliance, Madison proved to be a generally ineffective president, even though he won a second term in 1812. His cabinet appointments balanced sectional factions at the expense of competency. Relations with Congress proved rancorous. He confronted a group of War Hawks in the House—Henry Clay of Kentucky, John C. Calhoun from South Carolina, and Felix Grundy from Tennessee—who called for war with Britain. Old Democrat-Republicans, adherents of constrained government and states' rights, continued to be a thorn in Madison's side. In 1812 Congress refused to charter the Bank of the United States, even though Madison supported the measure as a financial necessity for a nation about to go to war. (Only when the government tottered toward bankruptcy in 1817 did Congress recharter a new bank.) The administration also lost control of its foreign policy when Congress enacted trade legislation that inadvertently favored Britain. Confronted by Britain's refusal to agree to recognize American neutrality and its continued support of Indian attacks on frontier settlers, Madison sent Congress a war message in June 1812, carrying the House seventy-nine to forty and the Senate by nineteen to thirteen.

War with Britain proved initially disastrous. The Democrats controlled Congress, intent on retiring the national debt and not raising taxes, and that left the army ill prepared. Madison's secretary of war proved utterly incompetent. In 1814, British forces attacked and burned the nation's young capital, Washington, D.C. Americans took solace in the courage and fortitude of Baltimore's Fort McHenry's resistance to a British bombardment, and they cheered a naval victory on Lake Champlain. When a final peace was reached at Ghent on Christmas Eve 1814, little had been achieved. Shortly before the final peace treaty arrived, Americans learned that Major General Andrew Jackson had defeated a British assault on New Orleans after the treaty had been negotiated.

Virginian James Monroe, another ally of Jefferson, won election to the presidency in 1816. By this time the Federalists had collapsed, having opposed the War of 1812 and threatened secession at a meeting in Hartford, Connecticut, shortly before the war concluded. The Hartford Convention proposed a two-thirds super-majority voting requirement in Congress for the admission of new states, declarations of war, and laws restricting trade. The convention also called for removing the three-fifths compromise that counted slaves as part of a state's population. News of Jackson's victory just a few weeks after the convention met spawned a patriotic fervor across the nation that discredited the Federalists, assuring their demise as a political force.

The war gave Americans a new hero—Andrew Jackson—and with him egalitarian democracy took root, organized around exactly what the Founders had feared: political parties.

Chapter 3
The age of democracy, 1816–44

In a single generation from 1816 to 1844, the United States underwent an economic, political, and social transformation. This market revolution occurred as a result of better transportation and communication systems. Canals, better roads, and new transportation via steamboats and railroads pushed farmers from subsistence agriculture to production for a vast national market. A communication revolution in print technology and the telegraph coincided with this transportation revolution. The development of a national postal system allowed widespread, easy distribution of newspapers. Handicraft industry increasingly gave way to factory production, especially in the textile and shoe industries. This boom occurred in a nation of twenty-four states and three territories reaching west to the Missouri River with a population of nearly 13 million people, triple the number in 1790.

This market revolution facilitated rapid political changes including the expansion of the electorate, the rise of political parties, and pronounced egalitarianism in campaign rhetoric. By 1825, voting restrictions based on property had been swept away in all but three states. None of the original states, with the exception of New Jersey, granted voting rights to women, and even this limited suffrage ended in 1807. Though barred from voting, women played a prominent role in politics, as activists in temperance, antislavery, prison reform, and other benevolent causes. Women found the new Whig party, which emerged in response to Jacksonian Democrats, particularly accommodating, as it systematically included them in campaign parades, rallies, and other events. Throughout the nation women were seen as the moral conscience of the nation.

By 1825, free blacks held voting privileges in only eight of the twenty-four states, and the number continued to decline in the following decades. Restrictions on female and free black voting coincided with the rise of propertyless (mostly urban artisans) white male suffrage. In 1825, only six states continued to have legislators pick presidential electors. Now they are chosen directly by voters.

Expressions of antielitism sometimes took peculiar forms. Following the murder of William Morgan in upstate New York after he threatened to reveal the secrets of the Masons, the Anti-Masonic party emerged. This party organized the first national party convention in American political history in 1832, although its strength rested mostly in upstate New York, Vermont, parts of Pennsylvania, and Ohio. Antielitism manifested itself also in more vile forms, including anti-Catholicism in print media and, occasionally, urban riots.

The political parties that emerged in the late 1820s and over the next decade gave voice to this egalitarian spirit. Both the Democratic and the new Whig parties proclaimed themselves representatives of the people. Newspapers proved essential to the development of political parties in this period when literacy rose to close to 80 percent. Newspapers proliferated: In 1789, there were about ninety; by 1829, about eight hundred. Most were local weeklies and highly partisan. Editors who did not follow the respective party line were removed.

The creation of a rudimentary two-party system increased participation among white male voters. At the same time, parties bolstered partisan spirit within the electorate. Election Days turned into great festivities, where free drinks, drunkenness, and violence were common. Party loyalty was reinforced by a polling system of voice votes in some localities, or ballots produced and distributed by candidates or parties in other places. Parties routinely printed ballots on colored paper, so they could tell which party's ballot was dropped in the ballot box. In these conditions, voters found it difficult to hide their affinities.

Political campaigning changed. Candidates projected themselves as "the common man," one of the people, not just someone running to represent the people. Campaigning resembled a kind of religious revival, which is not surprising because this was one of the great ages of religious revivalism in America, the so-called Second Great Awakening led by preachers such as Charles Grandison Finney. American politics always reflected moral passion combined with self-gain and economic and social interest, but these tendencies were intensified in this "age of democracy." This was an age of riots, and violent attacks against Catholics, Mormons, and Masons occurred.

In this age of party formation, politics often remained personal. For example, in Illinois coalitions, often dictated by personality and patronage, proved more important than party loyalty. Prior to becoming a state in 1819, Illinois instituted universal white male suffrage, making it the most democratic territory in the United States. As a territory, Illinois banned slavery and its Constitution prohibited reinstating it. Territories and young states such as Illinois became laboratories in democracy and imparted a raw democratic sentiment and egalitarianism on the frontier.

By the 1840s, professional politicians had built efficient organizations to conduct campaigns and rally voters. The turbulence of mass democracy and popular insurgency, however, limited the control that party managers could exercise. Political leaders spoke of "popular sovereignty" as the basis of legitimate political authority. Popular sovereignty found expression in having most government offices filled by election, in holding local, state, and national conventions, and in using mass conventions to pick candidates. Yet, even with the development of political parties, a strong antiparty sentiment continued to prevail inside both parties, especially the Whig party. As late as 1840, when Illinois Whigs began organizing county conventions, they refused to declare themselves "Whigs," but instead called for "Harrison supporters and reformers" to gather. In this call, Illinois Whigs projected their candidate William Henry Harrison as an antiparty reformer. Antiparty sentiment also surfaced in the periodic rise of antebellum third-party movements such as the Anti-Masonic Party, the Liberty Party, the Free Soil Party, and the Know-Nothing Party, each of which accused the established parties of corruption, self-interest, and control by alien forces, whether it be Masons, Catholics, or slaveholders.

Democrats and Whigs created national parties. In doing so, party leaders needed to smooth over ideological and sectional differences. New York politician Martin Van Buren—the "Little Magician"—allied the South and the Northeast through a program of limited government, states' rights, and low tariffs. Whigs backed Henry Clay's American System of a national bank, federally funded internal improvements, federal promotion of manufacturing interests, and high tariffs. In their competition to win sectional and regional support in the North, South, and expanding West, national party leaders avoided divisive issues, especially slavery. Until the 1850s, most political leaders and voters accepted the right to own slaves in the South, although whether slavery should be introduced into new territories or states proved a more controversial question.

Division over slavery appeared when Missouri applied for statehood early in James Monroe's administration. With the Federalist Party all but dead as a national party, politics remained confined within the

Democratic ranks. Ironically, Monroe's two presidential terms from 1817 to 1824 became known as the Era of Good Feelings, but political squabbling was far from over. In 1819, Missouri petitioned for statehood. Sectional conflict flared when a northern Congressman persuaded the House, where the populous North predominated, to amend an admission bill to prohibit bringing any new slaves into Missouri. The Senate, where the number of slave states and free states was even, rejected the amendment, but the debate continued into 1820. Many southerners, including Jefferson, were insistent that holding slaves was a constitutional right. Finally, Rep. Henry Clay of Kentucky stepped forward with a compromise that allowed for Maine, then part of Massachusetts, to be admitted as a free state and Missouri as a slave state. This compromise ensured parity between slave and free states in the Senate. As part of the Missouri Compromise, slavery was banned in the remaining Louisiana Purchase territory north and west of Missouri, along the 36° 30' parallel. The compromise barely passed the northern-dominated House. Monroe signed the legislation and easily won reelection in 1820, gaining all the electoral votes except one.

Immediately after Monroe's reelection in 1820, competition opened for his successor. All of the presidential hopefuls came out of Monroe's cabinet—with the single exception of war hero Andrew Jackson. Most viewed John Quincy Adams, the son of the former president, as the leading presidential contender. Adams, a former Federalist, brought to his candidacy a successful record as Secretary of State under Monroe. Jefferson, Madison, and Monroe had all served as Secretary of State before being elected president. Adams drafted the Monroe Doctrine, a presidential proclamation declaring American opposition to further European colonization in Latin America. He had been Monroe's only cabinet member to defend Jackson, who in an authorized attack on the Seminole Indians in Florida took it upon himself to execute two British nationals.

Other candidates were William Crawford, Secretary of the Treasury and a strict Jeffersonian and a states' rights man from

Georgia; Secretary of War John C. Calhoun, who enjoyed considerable support, but as a War Hawk in 1812 and a supporter of internal improvements, many people distrusted him; and Speaker of the House Henry Clay, who tried to build a base in the East and the West through his American System. From outside of Washington came Andrew Jackson, a hero of the war of 1812, who gained further fame when he led troops into Florida to quell Indian and runaway black slave incursions across the border.

Presidential politics was extremely fluid in 1824. The rules of the presidential game were uncertain, and politicians agreed that candidates should not appear to be campaigning. As a consequence, campaigns were conducted through newspapers and correspondence. The nomination process remained unclear. In the past a congressional caucus had nominated candidates, but denunciations of King Caucus were being heard. A few states held nominating conventions, but after Calhoun organized a convention in Pennsylvania, his campaign fizzled when the convention nominated Andrew Jackson. Calhoun withdrew to run unopposed for the vice-presidency. Crawford suffered a stroke, but his followers continued to press his candidacy. Clay stayed in the race hoping that a deadlocked House might turn to him. Everyone understood that none of the four candidates could win the Electoral College outright.

When the final electoral vote was counted, none of the candidates had a majority. Jackson stood the highest with ninety-nine; Adams followed with eighty-four, Crawford with forty-one, and Clay with thirty-seven. The Constitution provided that the House should elect one of the top three, so Clay's chances for the presidency were dashed, which may have been why Crawford's supporters kept him in the contest. Clay distrusted Jackson's states' rights views and threw his support to Adams after they met. With Clay's support, Adams won election. When Adams announced shortly afterwards that he was appointing Clay as Secretary of State (seen at the time as a step to the presidency), Jackson supporters denounced the election as a "corrupt bargain."

Adams came under immediate attack as soon as he stepped into the White House. A cold, temperamental man, he was not a natural politician. He was wealthy, spoke fourteen languages, and collected books, hardly an appealing figure to the common voter. He refused to listen to Clay, who urged Adams to make political appointments and to clear out incumbent government officials, especially in the postal system headed by John McLean, who directed local postmaster appointments to Jackson supporters. When Adams called for internal improvements including lighthouses, a national road, the establishment of a federally sponsored university, and a national observatory, his program drew charges of elitism.

Adams pursued contradictory policies. His exertions as Secretary of State to recover compensation from England for slaveholders who lost human property during the War of 1812, and his energetic evasions of British entreaties to cooperate in patrolling the seas for transoceanic slavers should have ingratiated him with the South. Adams saw protecting maritime commercial interests as good politics and good business, but he still did not garner Southern support. His position on Indian removal did not help with the South either. He wobbled at first. As Secretary of State he had advocated the removal of Indians to west of the Mississippi. As president he continued to believe that Indians could not be civilized, but came to believe that the Creek Nation in Georgia had been betrayed by their chiefs who had been bribed by land speculators. Adams eventually agreed to the removal of Creek Indians, but his earlier criticism had alienated many Southerners.

The midterm elections in 1826 gave Congress to Jackson's supporters. Vice President John C. Calhoun, who backed Jackson, joined with Senator Martin Van Buren to attack Adams. Van Buren engineered a tariff bill that set higher duties on many items, and the "Tariff of Abominations" particularly outraged Southern cotton planters. In this politicized environment, he became increasingly dejected, forgoing a once-vigorous exercise regimen of swimming in the Potomac River and walking five miles a day. Instead he sat for hours in his darkened office.

The 1828 election proved to be one of the nastiest in American history, with both sides launching vile personal attacks. Adams was charged with procuring an American virgin for the Czar's pleasure when he was ambassador to Moscow, while Jackson was accused of living out of wedlock with his beloved wife before she divorced her first husband. Opponents described Jackson's mother as a "common prostitute." On real issues Jackson and his followers were vague, even on the tariff. Called "Old Hickory" by his supporters, Jackson projected an image of a common man. Hickory Clubs and Central Committees supporting Jackson were organized across the country. In Pennsylvania, pro-Jackson pamphlets were published in German. Adams carried New England and other parts of the Northeast; Jackson, the South and West. Pennsylvania, with many Scots-Irish, and New York, with Martin Van Buren's political machine, proved critical to Jackson's election. He won 178 electoral votes to Adams's 83, and 56 percent to Adams's 43 percent in the popular vote.

The death of his wife, Rachael, following the election left the grieving Jackson embittered. He believed that campaign attacks on her had caused her death. Jackson came into office as a critic of elite corruption and a defender of Jeffersonian "Old Republicanism" that called for small, frugal government and states' rights. As a frontier Tennessee planter, slaveholder, Scots-Irish Presbyterian, and military general, Jackson brought to the White House strong, and sometimes vindictive, leadership. Through close advisers such as journalist Amos Kendall and Martin Van Buren, Jackson rewarded supporters with patronage jobs in government and fired opponents, sometimes on fabricated charges. He was a firm believer in the spoils system. Cabinet appointments reflected his insistence on party loyalty. His program aimed to improve the fortunes of his constituents—

white backwoods farmers, southern planters, and urban workers in the East.

Jackson's insistence on loyalty was evident when he demanded that members of his cabinet and their wives stop ostracizing Peggy Eaton, the wife of Jackson's campaign manager and Secretary of War John Eaton. Daughter of a tavern keeper, Peggy O'Neale Eaton exuded voluptuous sexuality and brought a sordid past from a previous marriage. The Eaton Affair so consumed Jackson that finally he forced his entire cabinet to resign, all except for Martin Van Buren, a widower who had befriended Peggy. Jackson selected Van Buren as his heir-apparent. The more substantive issue in Jackson's first administration was the removal of all Eastern Indians, including the Five Civilized Tribes of Cherokee, Creek, Choctaw, Chickasaw, and Seminole from Georgia, Alabama, and Mississippi. The Cherokee had received Western education, converted to Christianity, intermarried with whites, taken up cotton growing, and owned slaves. About 8 percent of the Cherokee families held slaves. Removing the Indians from lands desired by poor whites and land speculators proved to be good politics for Jackson. He disregarded complaints by Protestant missionaries, clergymen, and anti-Jackson congressmen including Senator Theodore Frelinghuysen of New Jersey and Clay. Jackson also willfully disregarded a Supreme Court decision upholding Indian rights.

The Indian Removal Act passed the House by only five votes. Shortly after, Jackson vetoed a major internal improvement measure, the Maysville Road Bill, which would have connected Kentucky with Ohio. Later he vetoed other internal improvement legislation, claiming that he supported internal improvements if they benefited the nation as a whole, such as river improvements and ports. As a result his administration actually spent more on internal improvements than previous administrations. These improvements often benefited cotton producers.

Jackson sought to make government more frugal, in order to pay off the national debt, which was accomplished in his administration. When it became clear that Jackson was not going to lower the tariff, Vice President John C. Calhoun secretly pushed the South Carolina legislature to resist tariff duties through a doctrine of nullification. This doctrine maintained that individual states could nullify any federal law. Although a believer in states' rights, Jackson was a nationalist. In a toast before Calhoun at a Democratic Party dinner, Jackson declared, "Our Union: It must be preserved." Jackson and Calhoun became bitter enemies. A defiant Calhoun took the nullification argument a step further in an anonymous pamphlet called the Fort Hill Address. Congress reduced the tariff in 1832, but South Carolina announced that the tariff was still too high and would not obey the law. Calhoun resigned as vice president, and Jackson replaced him in the 1832 election with Martin Van Buren. Only in 1833, after Jackson threatened to march personally with federal troops into South Carolina and hang Calhoun, did the state back down and suspend nullification of the tariff. Ironically, Henry Clay, Jackson's avowed enemy, arranged the compromise. Not all states' rights supporters, old Jeffersonians, supported Calhoun's doctrine that a single state could nullify a federal law, but this doctrine was to have important consequences for the nation.

Just prior to the election of 1832, another political controversy confronted the administration: Jackson's refusal to sign legislation rechartering the Second Bank of the United States. Nicholas Biddle, president of the bank, decided to bring rechartering up early to put Jackson on the political spot in an election year. Jackson disliked Biddle personally and politically for his support of paper money. Jackson believed the only legitimate money was gold or silver. He called the Second Bank an unconstitutional "hydra-headed" monster. When the bill came before him, Jackson, shown here in caricature, vetoed it in a message denouncing foreign investors and powerful banking interests. Jackson supporters rallied to the president's cause because they feared the

BORN TO COMMAND.

OF VETO MEMORY.

HAD I BEEN CONSULTED.

KING ANDREW THE FIRST.

3. This satiric image depicting Andrew Jackson as a king captures the fierce fight that followed his veto in 1832 of legislation to continue the Second National Bank. This veto led to the formation of the Whig Party and fierce partisan division in antebellum America.

bank's concentrated power. New York financial interests also disliked the Philadelphia-based bank.

Jackson's actions became the major campaign issue in 1832. Clay and his Whig supporters believed that the public favored the bank. Jackson tapped into a hatred of all banks shared by many, while appealing to entrepreneurs eager to start local banks. He won in a landslide.

In his second term, Jackson pursued a policy of destroying the Second Bank and instituting a hard-money policy. He ordered the removal of federal government deposits from the bank. When two treasury secretaries refused to remove the funds, Jackson forced them out and put Roger Taney in charge. He withdrew the funds and placed them in local "pet banks." (Taney was later rewarded by being appointed chief justice of the Supreme Court.) Jackson's policy ensured the dismantling of central banking in the United States for the rest of the century. Banks popped up across the country and issued their own paper currency. Inflation soared. Finally, Jackson issued the Specie Circular (1836) requiring federal debts, tariff duties, and land purchases to be paid in gold. The demand for gold (specie) forced the collapse of many banks and plunged the country into economic depression in 1837.

Van Buren received the Democratic Party nomination in 1836. The only discord at the second Democratic national convention appeared when western delegates placed Richard M. Johnson on the ticket. Johnson was a populist Kentuckian who claimed to have killed the Indian chief Tecumseh back in 1813. He drew support in the urban east among radical supporters of working men with his call to end debt laws. Many disliked Johnson because he openly lived with a mulatto slave woman.

A disorganized Whig opposition refused to call a national convention and instead put up three regional candidates, Indian fighter William Henry Harrison from Indiana, Hugh Lawson White from Tennessee, and Daniel Webster from Massachusetts. They centered the campaign on Van Buren's role as a sly manipulator in Jackson's autocratic administration. The campaign was conducted largely through stump speeches and publications. Tennessee Whig politician David Crockett, about to go off to Texas where he would die in the Alamo, authored a book in which he compared Van Buren to Jackson in terms of the analogy "dung to a diamond." Van Buren barely won 50 percent of the national popular vote, but took 170 electoral votes to the three Whig candidates' 113.

A national depression that began in 1837 ruined Van Buren's presidency. He exerted weak leadership in this crisis, even though Democrats controlled Congress. A prolonged and inconclusive war against the Seminole Indians, begun in Jackson's administration, added another burden to a frustrated Van Buren presidency. The mismanaged removal of Indians from the Southeast led to a "trail of tears" in which thousands died, generating outrage in the press. Van Buren's major accomplishment was the creation of an independent Treasury to receive federal funds. However, that action alienated many hard-core Jacksonians who feared any form of centralized banking.

Van Buren entered the 1840 race a wounded incumbent. Whigs smelled blood and this time put forward a single nominee, William Henry Harrison, who had been the strongest of the 1836 candidates and a war hero for defeating Indian leader Tecumseh at the battle of Tippecanoe. To balance the ticket, they selected states' rights Democrat John Tyler from Virginia, shouting "Tippecanoe and Tyler, Too." Whigs added to their ranks anti-Masons, such as Thurlow Weed and William H. Seward in New York and Thaddeus Stevens in Pennsylvania.

By 1840, both Democrats and Whigs were more ideologically coherent. Under Van Buren, Democrats became the party of hard money, although New York's workingmen's faction articulated more anticapitalist, antibanking views. Whigs still supported a new national bank, but they presented Harrison as a common man and Van Buren as an elitist. Clay told voters that the choice was between "the log cabin and the palace, between hard cider and champagne." Whigs distributed small log cabin containers filled with hard cider to voters. Campaign speeches, editorials, and pamphlets attacked Van Buren as anti-republican and aristocratic. Democrats countered with thousands of pamphlets and campaign biographies written for the occasion. Federal employees, census takers, postal employees, and customhouse clerks were called out to support of Van Buren. These efforts fell short as Harrison swept the Electoral College and won popular majorities in nineteen of twenty-four states.

Whigs won the White House using the Democratic playbook of a well-organized campaign, a sectionally balanced ticket, and a strategy of out-playing their opponents on the field of egalitarianism. Their success proved short-lived, however. Harrison died within a month of his inauguration. His vice president, Tyler, undermined the Whig program by refusing to charter a new national bank and vetoing legislation for internal improvements. As the election of 1844 approached, he tried unsuccessfully to win popular support by calling for the annexation of Texas, which had become independent from Mexico in 1836. The Texas issue threw American politics into a new world that disrupted Democrats and Whigs alike.

Chapter 4

The politics of slavery: prelude to the Civil War, 1844–60

Moral absolutes and democratic politics are not easily reconciled. By its nature, politics is the practice of compromise, and for those given to moral absolutes, compromise means betrayal of principle. The issue of slavery in late antebellum politics reveals this gap in tragic proportions. For many southerners, owning slaves was a property right upheld by the Constitution. For northern abolitionists, slavery denied the principle that all men—including blacks—were endowed with natural rights of liberty and equality before God. Of course, God's law was not easily determined by a majoritarian vote. In the 1850s, Abraham Lincoln, a principled and pragmatic Illinois politician, understood that a nation could not stand "half free and half slave."

In the ten years following the 1844 election the entire political landscape changed, including the demise of the Whig party and the rise of a powerful new northern party, the Republican Party. The catalyst for this dramatic political upheaval came from a single issue: slavery. New territories acquired at the end of the Mexican-American War unleashed a political crisis. The slavery issue divided the North and the South over the proper role of government. Southerners demanded a constitutional right to hold slaves and to extend slavery into the newly acquired territories. Slaveholders wanted government neutrality in protecting slavery in the South, while insisting that the federal government use coercive powers to return escaped slaves in the North to bondage in the South. Thus behind this insistence on states' right lay a contradictory notion of federal intervention in Northern states.

After Texas, the New Mexico territory, and California were acquired, the economy boomed. In this period of prosperity, large numbers of Irish and German immigrants poured into the country. The boom fostered the growth of manufacturing in cities in the North. At the same time cotton production soared in the South, which encouraged slavery. Ninety percent of the nation's manufactured goods, measured in value, came from the North. While only 3 percent of the white population in the South owned the majority of slaves, and only a third of white families owned slaves at all, the slave system became more entrenched economically and ideologically in that region. Fears of slave revolts intensified following a failed insurrection planned by Charleston free black Denmark Vesey in 1822 and an actual rebellion organized by slave Nat Turner in 1831 in which seventy or so of his followers killed fifty-seven whites in a house-to-house rampage. In the hysterical reaction caused by Turner's rebellion, it became impossible in the South to discuss ending slavery. Turner's rebellion, as well as escaped slave memoirs such as Frederick Douglass's *Narrative* (1845), Solomon Northup's *Twelve Years a Slave* (1853), and other accounts of slave resistance reinforced antislavery opinion in the North by expanding politics beyond simple party allegiance.

While slavery became entrenched in the South, antislavery sentiment in the North began to harden with a religious revival that swept the country in the 1830s. Believing that the millennium was approaching, evangelical Christians involved themselves in many areas of moral reform, including temperance, but slavery became the consuming issue for many by the late 1850s. The American Antislavery Society, organized in 1831 by religious abolitionists including William Lloyd Garrison and Theodore Weld and supported by the wealthy New York merchants Arthur and Lewis Tappan, claimed to have gained within a decade two hundred thousand members in two thousand local organizations across the North. Garrison's newspaper *The Liberator* encouraged radical abolitionism by demanding the immediate end of slavery and full civil rights for blacks. Free blacks such as Harriet Tubman, Sojourner Truth, and Frederick Douglass also crusaded for black freedom. Disdaining both Democrats and Whigs, many abolitionists refused to get involved in party politics, but their activities had profound political impact.

As radical abolitionism attracted a small, militant following, the movement produced violent reaction in the North in the 1830s and 1840s from mobs who attacked antislavery newspapers and editors (including killing Elijah Lovejoy in Alton, Illinois). In Congress, southerners prevented abolitionist petitions from being read or entered into the record. This so-called gag rule reinforced a perception that a "slave power" conspiracy controlled politics in Washington.

The Missouri Compromise of 1820 appeared at first to have resolved the issue of slavery in the territories by outlawing slaves north of the 36° 30' parallel. When Texas secured its independence from Mexico in 1836, the territorial slave issue once again became a flashpoint in American politics. John C. Calhoun, as President Tyler's secretary of state in 1845 and U.S. senator from South Carolina, led a campaign for the annexation of Texas. He and proslavery supporters introduced the annexation into the 1844 presidential election.

After the death of Harrison, Whigs naturally turned to Henry Clay, a guiding force in the Senate and the most popular person in the party. He resigned his Senate seat to devote himself full time to the 1844 campaign. The Kentuckian's nomination was a foregone conclusion. To balance the ticket regionally and ideologically with business-oriented Clay, the party selected a Christian evangelical, Theodore Frelinghuysen from New Jersey, as his running mate.

Van Buren emerged as the front-runner for the Democratic Party nomination. Although opposed to Texas annexation, former president Van Buren was the frontrunner. The pro-annexation Democrats, led by Calhoun, passed a new party rule requiring a nominee to get two-thirds of the delegates. This rule, repealed in 1936, gave the South veto over Democratic presidential candidates. At the convention, when it became clear Van Buren could never win two-thirds, delegates nominated dark horse James K. Polk, who enjoyed Andrew Jackson's support.

The 1844 election pitted Clay against Polk, but the abolitionist National Liberty Party nominated James G. Birney of Ohio. Clay hoped to avoid the Texas issue by focusing on his support for a high tariff. Polk promised to "reverse" the tariff, allowing his Pennsylvanian supporters to suggest an increase. While he pressed the Texas issue in the South, he proposed annexing all of Oregon in the North. As Clay's campaign sank in the South, he declared support for annexation and denounced abolition.

In an extremely tight race, Polk won the presidency. Clay lost the critical state of New York with thirty-six electoral votes by only five thousand votes. The Liberty Party received close to sixteen thousand votes, mostly from antislavery Whigs. If only a small number of these votes had gone to Clay, he would have won. Polk's dark-horse upset victory marked a major turning point in American political history.

On President Tyler's last day in office, Texas joined the union, although Mexico still refused to recognize Texas's independence or its boundaries. As an enthusiastic proponent of Manifest Destiny—America's destiny to extend from coast to coast— President Polk used diplomacy to negotiate with Britain the acquisition of the Oregon/Washington territory at the 49th parallel. Texas remained a thornier issue. Faced with an intransigent Mexico, understandably unwilling to dismember itself, Polk ordered U.S troops under Zachary Taylor to the north bank of the Rio Grande in the disputed territory between Texas and Mexico. The result was a military confrontation. Claiming that "American blood had been shed upon American soil," Polk persuaded Congress to declare war on May 13, 1846. By September of the following year, American forces stood outside the gates of Mexico City to force the conclusion of the war. In the peace treaty, Mexico recognized the Rio Grande as the Texas border and sold California and New Mexico to the United States. The Senate voted to ratify the treaty, despite objections from those who wanted to annex all of Mexico.

Fearing territorial expansion of slavery, northern Whigs were vociferous in opposing "Mr. Polk's War." At the beginning of the war, an obscure first-term Illinois congressman, Abraham Lincoln, having only recently arrived in Washington, proposed the "spot amendment" demanding that Polk show exactly where American blood had been shed on American soil. Northern Democrats divided on the issue. Some demanded that new territories should be opened to free white homesteaders. In June 1846, David Wilmot, a first-term congressman from Pennsylvania, introduced a proviso in Congress prohibiting slavery in any territory acquired in the war from Mexico. The measure passed the House on three occasions, only to be defeated in the Senate, which had a proslavery majority. Wilmot's proviso severely divided both parties sectionally. Partisan divisions, manageable through politics, were being replaced by sectional divisions.

The slavery issue in the new territories became the center of the 1848 presidential election. Polk upheld his campaign promise not to run for a second term. Under southern influence, Democrats nominated Lewis Cass, a northerner willing to support the South on slavery. Van Buren, who had been isolated by the Polk administration, denounced Cass as a "dough-face" candidate, a northerner willing to serve southern interests. After his delegates walked out of the national convention, Van Buren accepted the nomination of the Free Soil Party. Opposing expansion of slavery in the West under the slogan "Free Soil, Free Speech, Free Labor, and Free Men," the party selected Whig Charles Francis Adams, the son of the former president, as Van Buren's running mate, thus conjoining Jackson's former hand-picked successor and the son of his bitter enemy.

Remembering all too well the demise of the Federalists who had opposed the War of 1812, Whigs anxiously discarded their reputation as an antiwar party by nominating sixty-four-year-old "Rough and Ready" Zachary Taylor, a hero of the Mexican-American War. A career military officer, Taylor had never voted. Taylor ran with Millard Fillmore, a Buffalo lawyer who represented northern business interests. During the campaign, Taylor took no position on slavery in the territories. Northerners noted that his brother was an abolitionist in Ohio, while Southern Whigs observed that his wife had inherited slaves in Louisiana. Both parties tried to avoid the issue of slavery's extension and ignored Van Buren's Free Soil Party.

Whigs were jubilant when Taylor won the election. They now faced, though, the slave extension issue. Politically inept, Taylor satisfied no one when he proposed admitting both New Mexico and California to the union as states, while arguing that slavery in the territories should be left to the voters there. Ignoring Taylor, Henry Clay sought a grand bargain in Congress. His Omnibus Bill admitted California as a free state, which was consistent with public opinion there. New Mexico would be divided into Utah and New Mexico, with the expectation that Mormons in Utah would probably ban slavery, and New Mexico with its large Texas influence would adopt slavery. The United States would take over the Republic of Texas debt. Slavery would remain in the District of Columbia, but the slave trade would end. Most controversial was Clay's proposal to include a Fugitive Slave Law, which would require all free citizens to help recover runaway slaves. Asking Northerners to recover runaway slaves revealed a coercive state at its worst.

Clay's attempt at a compromise produced one of the greatest debates in Senate history. Daniel Webster of Massachusetts endorsed the bill, declaring he spoke not as a "northern man, but as an American." A dying John C. Calhoun denounced Clay's bill.

In early July 1850, Taylor suddenly died. His successor, Millard Fillmore, endorsed the compromise. At this point a young Democratic representative from Illinois, Stephen A. Douglas, stepped forward to break Clay's legislation into five separate bills that were enacted into law. Few members voted for the total package. The Compromise of 1850 proved to be the last and greatest contribution of Henry Clay and his generation. Calhoun died even before the debate concluded, and both Clay and Webster died two years later.

The Compromise of 1850 reflected a pragmatic balance of interests. Yet for all its careful construction it solved nothing, contrary to the expectations of most political leaders at the time who believed that the slavery issue had been put to rest. The Fugitive Slave Act angered many in the North, while the South was repulsed by northern denunciations of slavery.

With Fillmore too unpopular to be nominated in 1852, Whigs tried the old ploy of nominating a war hero, General Winfield Scott, to carry their banner. Whigs divided along sectional lines. The platform endorsed the Compromise of 1850, but Scott did not, a politically untenable position for a party's nominee. A fierce fight within the Democratic Party gave the nomination to New Hampshire politician Franklin Pierce, who won the nomination when an exhausted convention after forty-nine ballots finally settled on him as a compromise. His party managers convinced various delegates that he was "sound" on the compromise and would distribute patronage fairly (that is, not ignoring the South).

Scott, whose oldest daughter had converted to Catholicism, had hoped to court the Irish Catholic vote. His blatant catering to the immigrant vote stimulated anti-Catholicism and alienated growing nativist party members. Immigrant political opposition to temperance, a strong force in many Whig states, kept Irish and Germans loyal to the Democrats. Pierce crushed Scott, who carried only four states.

The magnitude of the defeat left the Whigs stunned. The Whig party began to break apart under the pressure of sectional differences, dissatisfaction of temperance and antislavery reformers, and anti-Catholic nativists who had become alienated from both existing parties. Democrats experienced these tensions as well, but having won the White House and control of Congress, the party felt a confidence their rivals lacked.

Party hubris bore its own seeds of destruction, however. Pierce, an alcoholic, proved to be politically incompetent. He angered supporters in New York by siding with the anti-Van Buren wing of the party. His pro-southern policies won him some support in the South but alienated others within the party. His greatest mistake was to support Stephen Douglas's Kansas-Nebraska Act in May 1854, one of the most fateful measures ever approved by Congress.

The measure promoted Douglas's concept of "popular sovereignty," which allowed the citizens of two new territories—Kansas and Nebraska—to vote to accept or reject slavery. Deferring to popular sovereignty expressed a democratic sentiment that voters within the states should decide the slave issue. The concept implied congressional neutrality on the slave issue in the territories, while making territories and states into laboratories of democratic governance. At the same time, the law repealed the provision in the Missouri Compromise of 1820 that no territory north or west of Missouri would ever have slavery.

Even before final passage the bill unleashed a firestorm of opposition in the North, opponents accused Douglas of serving the interests of the Slave Power—a label condemning southern influence in Washington. No doubt Douglas sought to win southern support in his bid to win the Democratic presidential nomination, but his main concern was to organize western territories to promote Chicago railroad interests that wanted to build a northern transcontinental railroad linking the East to the West.

Shocked by the reaction of northern public opinion against the act, party leaders were further jolted by the explosion of anti-Catholic, antiforeign hysteria that manifested itself in the summer of 1854 with the formation of the American Party. An outgrowth of a secret nativist party whose members refused to declare themselves in the open, the party was dubbed the Know-Nothings because when a member was asked about the party he was required to answer, "I know nothing." The party reflected the deep anxiety American Protestants felt with the largest influx of immigrants relative to the overall population in American history. Many of these immigrants were Irish and German Catholics. As a result, antislavery vied with nativism as the main issues before the American electorate. Both shattered old political alignments.

Antislavery leaders in the North sought to mobilize anti–Kansas-Nebraska Act voters through the formation of the new Republican Party, but the nativist movement complicated this plan. Events in Kansas, however, caused the American party itself to divide along sectional lines. In far-off Kansas, violence erupted as pro- and antislavery forces vied for control of the state government. In the first state election in 1855, proslavery forces gained control of the legislature through fraudulent voting. The proslavery legislature enacted draconian measures making it a felony to maintain that slavery did not legally exist in the territory, or even to print antislavery material. Further outrages in Kansas, fanned by the abolitionist press, spurred antislavery opinion in the North.

The establishment of the Republican Party came in fits and starts. It coalesced around a heterogeneous coalition of Christians and free-thinking Germans, temperance supporters and antiprohibitionists, Free Soil Democrats and former Whigs, Yankee business leaders, farmers, and urban workingmen fearful of competition from slave labor.

Events in Kansas fostered the growth of the sectionally based Republican Party. Douglas's concept of popular sovereignty in Kansas turned into a bloody nightmare, a failed experiment for states as a laboratory for democracy. As the election of 1856 approached, the antislavery forces in Kansas organized the free-state government in Topeka. In response, the proslavery chief justice of the state ordered the arrest of free slavery leaders and the closing of two free-state newspapers in Lawrence. A proslavery sheriff and posse, against the advice of even many proslavery men, entered the free-state town of Lawrence, arrested many antislavery leaders, destroyed two newspaper presses, and burned the Free State Hotel. Only one person was killed in the attack, but press reports of the "sacking of Lawrence" inflamed northern opinion. When abolitionist and religious fanatic John Brown retaliated for the Lawrence raid by killing a family of alleged proslavery men living in Pottawatomie, he was greeted as a hero in some northern circles.

In the Senate, abolitionist Charles Sumner rose to deliver an attack on the administration in a speech entitled "The Crime against Kansas." Shortly after that May 1856 speech, a South Carolina congressman, Preston S. Brooks, entered the Senate chamber and beat the seated Sumner over the head with a cane until he was unconscious. Brooks believed southern honor was at stake in Sumner's verbal abuse of the venerated senator from South Carolina, Andrew P. Butler, who was Brooks's uncle. The attack on Sumner, in the very halls of the Senate, electrified northern opinion, who heard of the Sack of Lawrence the next day. Brooks resigned his seat, only to be triumphantly reelected. The ladies of Charleston presented Brooks with a silver-headed cane inscribed, "Hit him again."

Almost overnight the presidential campaign had been transformed. The events of May wrecked any chance Pierce might have had for a second term. When the faction-ridden Democratic Party met, it picked James Buchanan as standard-bearer. As ambassador to England during the Pierce presidency, Buchanan had avoided the controversy over the Kansas-Nebraska Act. An old Federalist who had switched to the Democratic Party, Buchanan, a bachelor whose brief marriage had ended in an annulment, brought stately appeal to party factions. The American (Know-Nothing) party went with former president Millard Fillmore, who tried to temper the party's antiforeign rhetoric. (Many Know-Nothing candidates lower on the ballot declared themselves antislavery men.) Republicans turned to forty-three-year-old John C. Frémont, a political unknown, who had gained national fame as a western explorer. He was also the son-in-law of Thomas Hart Benton, who endorsed Buchanan. During the campaign, Democrats attacked Frémont as having secretly converted to Roman Catholicism, his wife's faith. Frémont was an Episcopalian, but Republicans found themselves unable to deal successfully with this attack.

The 1856 presidential campaign swept northern voters into delirious excitement, leading one veteran Indiana politician to observe that "Men, Women & Children seemed to be out with a kind of fervor." Especially notable were young voters who rallied to the Republican cause. An estimated 83 percent of the northern electorate went to the polls in 1856. In the end, Buchanan was an easy victor in the Electoral College, although he failed to win the majority of the popular vote with 45.3 percent compared to Frémont's 33.1 percent and 21.6 percent for Fillmore. Buchanan's sweep of the Southern vote proved crucial to his election. This confirmed his opponents' view of him as at heart a southern man dressed in northern garb.

Further events assured that slavery became the dominant issue in American politics, which played to the strength of the nascent

Republican Party. The critical question facing it was selection of a viable presidential candidate. The party found that man in a former Whig congressman, Abraham Lincoln. In 1858 few in the East knew Lincoln, but Illinoisans found in this small-town successful lawyer a gifted politician who combined principle and pragmatism, eloquence and humility, and intelligence without pretense. He gained national attention when he challenged Stephen Douglas for reelection to his Senate seat in 1858.

In a series of debates that took the candidates throughout the state, covered by the national press, the two men squared off in one of the most engaging contests in American history. Lincoln challenged Douglas's concept of popular sovereignty by maintaining that blacks possessed natural rights set down in the Declaration of Independence that made them equal as men. Lincoln believed government should protect natural rights by serving as a referee of sectional interests. Douglas ably defended his views, although he played to the racist sentiments of the tens of thousands who turned out for the debates by accusing Lincoln of believing in racial intermarriage. He accused Lincoln of refusing to recognize the legality of the Dred Scott decision. The case involved a freedom suit by a former slave, Dred Scott, whose owner had brought him into free federal territory in Iowa. Instead of ruling on the narrow merits of the case, Chief Justice Roger Taney, a Jackson appointee, ruled that slave ownership was a constitutional right based on property rights. This decision opened the possibility of establishing slavery in every federal territory and state. After it, many in the North concluded that Supreme Court failed in its role as a fair referee.

Lincoln won the popular vote, but he lost the Senate seat because Democrats held a narrow margin in the malapportioned legislature that actually picked the senator. The campaign brought Lincoln, shown on the next page in a campaign banner from his 1860 presidential bid, to national attention. In other states, Republicans made huge gains in Congress.

Emotions ran high in both the North and South by the time of the 1860 election. Passions had been inflamed by an unsuccessful attempt a year earlier when John Brown, already notorious for his Kansas killings, conspired with a small group of northern abolitionists to launch a slave uprising by raiding a federal armory in Harpers' Ferry, Virginia. Brown was captured, tried by Virginia for treason, and executed in front of a howling Southern mob. Although the raid was denounced by leading politicians, including Lincoln, Brown was made into a martyr by northern abolitionists, which reinforced southern fears of the North. By this time, firebrands in the South and North called for force to protect what they saw as fundamental rights—states' rights versus human rights.

At the Chicago Republican convention in 1860, backers of Abraham Lincoln skillfully won the nomination of their candidate

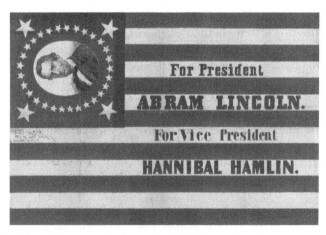

4. This cotton campaign flag used in the 1860 election casts a misspelled Abraham (Abram) Lincoln and his running mate, Hannibal Hamlin, as defenders of the Union against Southern secessionists. The thirteen stripes in the banner represent the founding states of the nation.

over New York's William Seward. The party platform stressed antislavery and free labor, acceptance of slavery in the South, but not the territories, a high tariff to benefit manufacturers and urban workers, the building of a transcontinental railroad, and a homestead act giving farmers free federal land.

The Democrats, the remaining national party, divided at their convention in Charleston, South Carolina. After 57 ballots the convention adjourned without nominating a candidate. Northern Democrats met to nominate Stephen Douglas. A few days later southern Democrats picked John Breckinridge of Kentucky. Meanwhile, a third group, the Constitutional Union Party, composed of conservative southern Whigs and Know-Nothings, nominated John Bell of Tennessee. While the election had four candidates, the race came down to two sectional contests, Lincoln and Douglas in the North and Breckinridge and Bell in the South. Douglas broke precedent by traveling the country to campaign.

On Election Day, Lincoln swept the North, where he gained 55 percent of the vote. He won the Electoral College. Douglas's only victory came in the border state of Missouri. Lincoln's campaign reflected a well-organized Republican Party on the state and local levels, which brought many new voters to the polls. In the South, Constitution Party nominee Breckinridge, defending the right of slaveholders to take slave property any place in the United States, defeated Bell. The election of an antislavery Republican president outraged the South. On December 20, 1860, South Carolina seceded from the Union. A lame duck Congress debated how to solve the crisis with a compromise. Meanwhile, a powerless Lincoln waited to be inaugurated. He would soon be tested by the worst crisis ever faced by the young nation.

Chapter 5
Politics in war and Reconstruction, 1861–76

The Civil War and its aftermath intensified politics in the North, sharpening the divide between Republicans and Democrats and factionalizing the Republican Party. The war did not politically unite the North during the war. Abraham Lincoln confronted deep factionalism in his own party and a Democratic Party calling for peace with the rebel Confederates. Within his own party, Lincoln faced opposition from Radical Republicans who insisted upon emancipation of slaves and vengeance on the South. Conservative Republicans called for caution. These factional divisions worsened after Lincoln's assassination in 1865, leading the Republican Congress to impeach its own party leader, Andrew Johnson, who succeeded Lincoln in the White House.

In April 1861, just a month after Lincoln's inauguration, South Carolina, acting under orders from Confederate President Jefferson Davis, fired on the federally manned Fort Sumter in Charleston Harbor. Following the attack, the important state of Virginia voted to join the deep southern slave states in forming a new Confederacy. Arkansas, Tennessee, and North Carolina announced their secession from the Union, but the slave states of Delaware, Maryland, Kentucky, and Missouri stayed in the Union. The Civil War had begun. Both sides proved wrong in expecting a short war. The war lasted four bloody years; there were 750,000 casualties by most recent estimates.

Both the North and the South believed they were upholding the Constitution. The Confederates modeled their new government on the Constitution. The Confederate president, Jefferson Davis, based in the new capital in Richmond, led a one-party regime, but faced continued opposition from a few vociferous state governors who complained about his authoritarian policies. For Northern unionists, Southern secession betrayed the principles of democracy by overturning the results of a legitimate election.

Lincoln's primary concern in the beginning of the war was to keep the border slave states from joining the rebellion. One consequence of this strategy was that he needed to tread lightly on the slave question. At the same time, northern opponents of the war, labeled by Lincoln followers as snakelike Copperheads, vigorously attacked Lincoln's war policies and called on their followers not to support the war. In response, Lincoln undertook drastic measures, including arrests of newspaper reporters, editors, and opposition leaders, and the suspension of habeas corpus. Government and military officials suppressed Copperhead newspapers such as the *New York News* and the *Chicago Times*. Lincoln justified his actions on constitutional powers of the commander-in-chief.

Republicans came into power on the high idealistic promise of "free soil, free labor, and free men." This belief in economic opportunity was expressed in legislation to provide free western land to settlers in the Homestead Act (1862) and federal funding of a transcontinental railroad from Omaha to Sacramento, and to support colleges through the Morrill Act (1862). Republicans enacted a high protective tariff to support American manufacturing. While some of these laws benefited the nation as a whole, special interests often took advantage of such legislation for their own personal gain. While expressing high ideals, Republicans pursued "politics as usual" during the war.

Neither northern Republicans nor northern Democrats fully accepted a two-party system. After all, by 1861, Americans had witnessed political parties come and go over for some seventy years—the Federalists, the Whigs, and the Know-Nothings. The concept of "loyal opposition" found little expression within either political party. Conspiracy theories prevailed in both. Politically aligned newspapers, 1,300 in the North, provided a continual source for these alleged conspiracies. Democratic papers reported that Lincoln and his allies were planning a military coup. Throughout the war, Republicans issued warnings against conspiracies by such pro-Confederate groups operating in the North, such as the Knights of the Golden Circle and Sons of Liberty. Later historians question how active these organizations actually were.

Within the new Republican Party, patronage, corruption, and bribery remained mainstays. By the war's end, the federal government had grown to 53,000 employees, making it the largest employer in the nation. A new pension system for Union veterans and their dependents, established in 1865, created huge patronage opportunities for the party, by ensuring the Northern veteran votes. With patronage came unavoidable corruption. The New York Customs House was a perennial problem. In Pennsylvania, the former secretary of war, Simon Cameron, driven from the cabinet for incompetence and corruption, tried to bribe his way into the Senate in 1862. In response, some opponents threatened Democratic state legislators with assassination if they bolted to Cameron, who was playing both sides of the aisle. Democrats won the seat in the end, but old-style power politics, intrigue, and factionalism prevailed in Pennsylvania, as it did in Illinois, Indiana, and many other states.

Even in the midst of a Civil War, elections continued. During the forty-eight-month duration of the Civil War, Americans went to the polls for local, state, and national elections at least half of those months. Americans lived and ate politics. Political rallies often lasted all afternoon, characterized by debates over resolutions, oratory, and singing. Political activity took more violent forms as well, as mobs broke into newspaper offices.

In July 1863, mob activity—stimulated by the Confederate secret service—manifested itself most vilely in a week-long riot in New York City. This race riot, mostly by Irish Catholic working-class men and women, turned into the largest insurrection in American history at the time. Much of this anger was directed toward free blacks living in the city. Rioters murdered hundreds of people and burned to the ground fifty buildings, including two Protestant churches and a black orphanage. Federal troops arriving from the Gettysburg battle finally suppressed the riot.

At the same time, the war invigorated reform. Women in particular became involved in voluntary activities through the U.S. Sanitary Commission, which offered medical relief to soldiers, and the freedmen's aid movement, which helped provide government relief to destitute freed slaves. Hundreds of thousands of women participated in local societies raising money, supplies, and books for soldiers and freed blacks. These activities produced a postwar generation of women leaders found in urban charity and the Woman's Christian Temperance Union. In the North, black ministers, abolitionists, and professional men organized to improve conditions of northern blacks. These efforts led Massachusetts in 1865 to enact the first comprehensive public accommodations law outlawing segregation. New York City, San Francisco, Cincinnati, and Cleveland desegregated their streetcars during the war. Less successful were efforts in the North to give voting rights to blacks.

In the first two years of the war, 1861–62, it went poorly for Union forces as they suffered major military defeats. This heightened opposition in the North among Democrats and Republicans about Lincoln's conduct of the war. Lincoln's greatest political success in the first years was containing further secession in the border states. Military occupation of western Virginia allowed the creation of a new state that elected a new governor and sent two senators and three representatives to Washington. Military authorities reorganized Maryland's and Missouri's governments.

In Missouri, which was under martial law, Union commander and former presidential candidate John C. Frémont issued an edict, threatening to court-martial and execute civilians in arms, confiscate property of those who aided the enemy, and free the slaves of rebels. Fearing that this order might push border states to rebellion, Lincoln ordered the general to bring his order in line with the Confiscation Act enacted by Congress, which allowed, through judicial proceedings, the confiscation and freeing of slaves of those assisting the rebellion. Lincoln's countermand stirred up widespread protest among radical abolitionists in the North.

In late 1862, as the war continued to go poorly, Lincoln issued the preliminary Emancipation Proclamation that promised to free slaves of rebels in Confederate states. This limited measure served military purposes and expressed Lincoln's deep belief that the war was about freeing the slaves. Press notices about the forthcoming proclamation aroused Democratic opponents and cheered the radical wing of Lincoln's own party. Shortly after the draft of the proclamation began to be circulated in the northern press, Lincoln suspended the right of habeas corpus, the right to appear before a court after an arrest. In September, Lincoln declared that all slaves in states in rebellion would be free and authorized the enlistment of blacks into the army. The proclamation and the suspension of habeas corpus cost Lincoln votes in the midterm elections of 1862. On New Year's Day 1863, he signed the final proclamation of emancipation. He believed that the war was about preserving the union and ending slavery. Lincoln had finally acted to free slaves in the rebel states.

The failure of the war effort, rising inflation, charges of corruption, and suspension of habeas corpus revived the Democratic Party in the North in the 1862 midterm elections, especially in Pennsylvania, Ohio, Indiana, and New York. The Emancipation Proclamation won Republicans some support in New England, but played poorly among Irish voters in the urban

East and lower Midwest. Democrats took control of states across the lower North. In New York, Democrat and fierce Lincoln opponent Horatio Seymour won the governorship against a badly divided Republican Party. Democrats won thirty-five congressional seats, including Lincoln's home district of Springfield, Illinois. Because of succession, Republicans still held control of Congress, but the election losses revealed that the Democratic Party—the party of traitors in the eyes of Republicans—was not going the way of the Federalists in 1812.

Even after the war began to turn more favorably toward the union in 1863, political fighting continued, as bitter as ever, reaching a peak in the 1864 presidential election. Lincoln entered his campaign for reelection convinced that he would lose. Union forces had suffered military defeats, and the Republican Party stood ideologically divided. Radical Republicans expressed discontent with Lincoln's mild approach to reconstruction. Disillusioned with Lincoln, Radical Republicans met in Cleveland in May 1864 to form a new party called Radical Democracy to nominate John C. Frémont. But his campaign quickly fizzled with lack of support. He withdrew from the race in September, declaring that winning the war was too important to divide the Republican Party.

Democrats turned to General George B. McClellan, who had built the Union army in the east, chased Confederate general Robert E. Lee all over Virginia, failed to take Richmond, and was fired by Lincoln. The party platform urged accommodation with the Confederacy. Democrats, however, were far from united. A group of War Democrats broke with the party to join Republicans to organize the National Union Party. Opposition to Lincoln's nomination formed around journalist Horace Greeley, Senator Benjamin Wade, and Secretary of the Treasury Salmon P. Chase. Lincoln's popularity within the Republican Party forced Chase to withdraw his challenge, allowing Lincoln to win the nomination. He replaced Vice President Hannibal Hamlin with a new running mate, Andrew Johnson, a War Democrat and military governor of

Tennessee, and temporarily renamed the party the Union Party. The slogan, "Don't change horses in the middle of a stream," captured the general mood of the country. Lincoln centered his campaign on emancipation. Republican state parties stressed the treason of antiwar Northern Democrats.

Secretary of State and Lincoln confidant William Seward set the tone for the 1864 election in a speech entitled "The Allies of Treason," given shortly after news that Democrats had nominated George B. McClellan for president and that Atlanta had fallen to General William T. Sherman. Republican charges of cowardice and treason were matched by Democratic rhetoric of moral corruption and miscegenation, a newly invented word to describe interracial marriage. New female employees in the Treasury Department were accused of engaging in prostitution. The nation's capital, Washington, D.C., had become "the Sodom of America" under Republican rule. Lincoln's policy of using black troops became a symbol for these opponents of a perceived nation in decline. They warned that financing the war through the printing of paper money would bring economic decline to the nation.

Lincoln defeated McClellan in the general election. He was aided by Democratic Party division, the fall of Atlanta in September, and the soldier vote. Twenty-five states participated in the election. McClennan won only three: Kentucky, Delaware, and his home state of New Jersey. Lincoln swept the others, winning 55 percent of the popular vote and 212 electoral votes. Massachusetts Senator Charles Sumner declared the Democratic Party dead: "It was no longer patriotic.... It should no longer exist." Sumner's remark revealed that the concept of two-party competition was not widely accepted among Republicans. Moderation was not a part of politics, before and during, the Civil War.

In his second term, Lincoln feared that his Emancipation Proclamation might be overturned by a hostile judiciary, so he undertook to enact the federal Thirteenth Amendment to the

Constitution, ensuring that blacks be guaranteed permanent freedom. He brought it before Congress in late 1863 to formally abolish slavery throughout the United States. Radical Republicans led by Senator Sumner and Pennsylvania Representative Thaddeus Stevens wanted a more expansive amendment but were defeated in committee. Lincoln, working with William Seward and friendly congressmen, instructed that all stops be pulled out to ensure passage of the amendment. All stops meant patronage, political pressure, and outright bribes. He also made direct appeals to win over reticent House members.

The president sought to reconcile the nation through allowing Confederate states to rejoin the Union once 10 percent of the population of a rebellious state pledged to support the union and accept emancipation. Lincoln's pragmatic approach to postwar reconstruction sought to reconcile the South, while ending slavery forever. The Radical Republican wing feared that former Confederates would gain control of reconstructed states and suppress the newly won rights of freed slaves. Tensions became evident when Lincoln used a pocket veto of the Wade-Davis bill in July 1864, which made readmission to the union contingent on 50 percent of a state's population swearing loyalty to the Union.

On April 14, 1865, Lincoln was assassinated by a white supremacist southern fanatic, John Wilkes Booth. Whether the politically skilled Lincoln might have prevailed over Radicals in his own party cannot be known. Nor can we know if Lincoln would have taken more coercive measures to protect the rights of freed slaves under violent attack by whites anxious to maintain power and privilege. What is certain, though, is that his successor, Andrew Johnson, ran into a buzz saw in Congress. The radical wing of the Republican Party emerged ascendant following Lincoln's death. Driven by antislavery idealism and a conviction to win the peace and to protect freed blacks from white violence, Radical Republicans sought to crush any revival of the Democratic South and to complete a social transformation of the former slave states.

The most important political consequence of the Civil War and Reconstruction proved to be the transformation of slaves into equal citizens of the nation. Congress enabled this through constitutional amendments—the Thirteenth, Fourteenth, and Fifteenth—which abolished slavery, granted equal citizenship, and protected voting rights for former slaves. These amendments, as well as new civil rights legislation, altered federal-state relations. The four million men and women freed from slavery discovered opportunities for political and civic involvement in the North and the South. The struggle to fulfill these rights and to engage in civic life brought political acrimony at every level of government, national, state, and local. Many black leaders in the South gained their first experience as Union soldiers to become active in organizing Union Leagues tied to the Republican Party throughout the South.

Andrew Johnson proved tone-deaf to public opinion and Congress. His major political goal, it seemed, was to break the political control of the southern aristocracy, yet his policies faced opposition from congressional Radical Republicans for being too lenient toward the South. In 1865, he issued proclamation pardons for all southern rebels willing to sign loyalty oaths. Excluded from this general amnesty program were Confederate officials and owners of taxable property worth more than $20,000, who had to apply individually for presidential pardons. Many of the restored southern state legislatures enacted Black Codes sharply curtailing basic rights of black freedmen. These new codes imposed harsh labor regulations that were intended to maintain planter hegemony and, in effect, instituting a new form of forced labor. For example, in Mississippi black laborers leaving their jobs before the contract expired were required to forfeit all wages earned previously.

Reports of violent intimidation of blacks by newly organized white groups such as the Ku Klux Klan further outraged the North. Opponents of Republican-dominated reconstructed state legislatures noted that special interests used bribery to win charters for railroads, urban streetcar franchises, mineral rights, banking, and manufacturing, to the dismay of reformers. Critics of southern Reconstruction tended to overlook urban corruption in the North.

At the core of Radical Republicanism lay a civic ideology grounded in American citizenship and equal rights. Radical Republicans, however, remained divided on black suffrage. They were committed to "loyal" government, a free labor economy, and protection of freedmen's basic rights. The widespread belief of congressional Republicans that the federal government needed to shoulder responsibility for the newly freed slaves was symbolized in the creation of the Freedmen's Bureau in 1865, charged with aiding blacks in the South. In addition, Congress passed a Civil Rights bill in 1866 to protect the legal rights of all citizens through federal oversight. President Johnson surprised Congress when he vetoed both bills. This proved to be a major political mistake.

Congress pushed forward, overriding Johnson's vetoes. Using their overwhelming majority in Congress, Radical Republicans passed the Fourteenth Amendment providing citizenship rights and legal protection to all male citizens. Johnson believed that Radicals had misjudged public opinion, and he denounced them in the midterm elections in 1866. On the campaign trail, his harsh attacks and vituperative language, best suited to Tennessee stump speeches, dismayed friends and the general public. Reminding voters of the war's high cost by literally waving blood-soaked shirts at rallies, Radicals won large majorities in Congress in 1866, ensuring a clash with Johnson.

In 1867 Congress passed—over Johnson's veto—the Reconstruction Act establishing five military districts covering ten ex-Confederate states (Tennessee had been readmitted). Under the law and supplemental measures, twenty thousand federal troops, including black units, were assigned to the districts. Southern states were required to adopt new constitutions drafted by conventions elected by universal male suffrage. The U.S. Army registered voters. Former federal officers and high-ranking Confederate soldiers who had supported the rebellion were barred from participation, and blacks formed a majority of registered voters in Alabama, Florida, Louisiana, Mississippi, and South Carolina. In South Carolina, Mississippi, and Louisiana, Republicans prevailed because of large black majorities among the electorate. Republican Party leaders in these states were mostly white, but black leaders increasingly demanded their share of leadership and patronage positions. By 1868 Congress had approved new state constitutions and readmission into the Union of former Confederate states in time for the coming presidential election.

Radicals moved to impeach President Johnson when he attempted to remove Secretary of War Edwin Stanton from the cabinet in violation of dubious legislation passed by Congress forbidding presidential removal of cabinet officers. As impeachment proceedings progressed, public opinion as well as business leaders reacted unfavorably to the arrogance of Congress. The widely disliked president pro-tem of the Senate, Benjamin Wade of Ohio, would become president if Johnson was removed. He was acquitted, 35 to 19, one vote short of conviction, when seven Republicans joined Democrats in opposing removal.

Johnson hoped that Democrats might nominate him in 1868. Instead, a divided convention finally turned to New York governor Horatio Seymour, a pro-southern and anti-Reconstruction politician. Republicans went with northern war hero Ulysses S. Grant, a military career officer, who had not previously shown much interest in partisan politics. The Republican platform called for the continuation of Radical Reconstruction and black suffrage in the South, but left the issue of black suffrage in the North to the states. Following tradition, Grant did not actively campaign, but promised, "Let us have peace." He swept the Electoral College, although the popular vote was much closer. Grant's victory was aided by the black vote through the enactment of the Fifteenth Amendment giving blacks voting rights. Republicans carried all the southern states except Georgia and Louisiana, but the majority of the total white vote in the North and the South went to Seymour.

Grant pursued a contradictory policy of trying to reconcile white southerners, while using the army to protect black rights. In doing so, he alienated members of his own party and Democrats. In the South, Republicans broke into factions. A few opportunistic white southerners joined the Republican Party, but most stuck with the Democrats. In Georgia, Governor Joe E. Brown, a former Confederate-turned-Republican, sought to expel blacks from the party. Seeking to reduce black influence in the legislature, he moved the state capital from Milledgeville in the heart of the black belt to Atlanta, a railroad-dominated town. Throughout the South, white vigilante movements used violence to intimidate black and white Republican voters. More than a few blacks fled the South to northern cities or to found their own communities in Kansas.

By 1872, it was clear that Radical Reconstruction was in decline. Even liberal reformers such as newspaper editor Horace Greeley proved willing to retreat from it. The longtime reformer loathed the era's sleazy, crooked politics apparent in both the North and the South. Disgusted with Grant, liberal Republicans broke ranks to form the new Liberal Republican Party, which nominated Greeley as their candidate for president. Democrats, hoping to split the Republican vote, endorsed Greeley as their candidate in a strange coalition of liberal reformers and Democrats. Reformers such as Henry Adams, crusading editor of *The Nation*, historian and grandson of the former president John Quincy Adams, backed Greeley.

The campaign proved once again to be nasty. Greeley was attacked as a traitor. Thomas Nast, a nationally prominent cartoonist, depicted Greeley as extending his hand to Lincoln's assassin, John

Wilkes Booth. Democrats charged Grant with being a military dictator for sending federal troops to Louisiana through the Martial Act. Although divided, Republicans prevailed, electing Grant to a second term.

Grant's second term was marred by an economic crash in 1873 and corruption. Insider trading in the gold market reached into the White House, involving Grant's personal secretary. Revelations of a Whiskey Ring, in which distillers bribed Treasury officials to evade liquor taxes, further damaged the administration. In 1872, numerous prominent Republicans in Congress were discovered to have accepted stock from Crédit Mobilier, a dummy corporation set up for the Union Pacific Railroad, which had been given huge land grants by Congress. Grant's political problems worsened when Democrats gained control of the House in the midterm 1874 elections.

Scandal, political corruption, and economic depression played to Democrats as they entered the 1876 election. The party nominated New York reformer Samuel Tilden, a Wall Street lawyer. Republicans nominated Rutherford B. Hayes, an Ohio politician and the husband of a leading temperance reformer. Tilden won the popular vote, but the electoral vote was so close that it came down to disputed votes in South Carolina, Florida, and Louisiana, that if counted for Hayes gave him the election. Both parties submitted "official returns" from the three states. Southern white Democrats challenged these votes and prepared to seize power through force. A divided Congress with a Democratic-controlled House and a Republican Senate turned the election deadlock into a national crisis. Finally, after a secret meeting of Republican and southern Democratic leaders, a special commission was established with eight Republicans and seven Democrats who reached a grand compromise that gave the election to Hayes. Democrats were allowed to "win" the state election in three states. The eventual withdrawal of federal troops allowed Southern states to suppress the rights of blacks as citizens.

The Republic had survived the Civil War and Reconstruction. Slavery had been abolished and blacks gained constitutional rights as citizens. During Reconstruction, blacks got their first taste of political involvement. During the war, women gained political experience on the national level, although they still lacked voting rights. The South became heavily Democratic, and Republicans became an established party. Two-party competition remained intact, warts and all.

A civil war challenged the constitutional order of the republic, but in the end, at great expense, the Constitution remained the foundation of the nation. Rights of citizenship and voting rights had been granted to black men, and however constricted by state rule, these rights were now embedded in the Constitution awaiting full implementation by future generations.

Chapter 6
Gilded Age frustration and the Progressive response, 1877–1918

Self-gain, partisan loyalty, and corruption characterized politics after the Civil War at a time when United States became the world's leading industrial power. From 1877 through 1900, Americans—white males—participated in politics as never before. Voters divided generally along ethnic, religious, and sectional lines. Republicans controlled the White House during most of these years, while party control of Congress remained divided, with the Republicans usually holding the Senate and Democrats the House.

During the late nineteenth century, the presidency remained weak, in large part because of the mediocrity of most who held it. The emergence of a Progressive movement in the first decades of the twentieth century strengthened the executive office, enlarged federal power, and marked the beginnings of the regulatory administrative state. Government became more interventionist, exerting its coercive powers to tax, protect workers and consumers, and oversee national monetary policy. Politics remained as fierce as ever, but the call for nonpartisan government and the emergence of newspapers and magazines not directly controlled by political parties helped change the tenor. Even though suffrage expanded to include women, voter turnout declined in part because of new voting regulations and general apathy within the electorate.

After the Civil War, political machines in both parties dominated politics in the North. The South remained solidly Democratic. These machines, controlled by political bosses, often showed flagrant disregard for public morality. Politicians ignored problems created by the new industrial order and urban dislocation, and numerous third parties were unsuccessful in challenging politics as usual. By 1900 middle-class Americans, fed up with corruption and the failure to address social issues, backed progressive reformers inside both political parties. Progressivism began on the local and state levels, but also produced three reform-minded presidents, Theodore Roosevelt, William Howard Taft (to a lesser degree), and Woodrow Wilson. With reform came a stronger presidency and the growth of the federal government.

The problems of late nineteenth-century America seemed embodied in the presidency. Republicans controlled the White House throughout this period, except for the election of Democrat Grover Cleveland in 1884 and 1892. Following the Compromise of 1877, Republican Rutherford B. Hayes, a Civil War hero and devoted family man, entered the White House even though he lost the popular vote. His morally earnest wife, Lucy, a teetotaler, refused to serve alcohol in the White House, much to the dismay of congressmen and foreign dignitaries.

Hayes stepped into an economic depression that created massive unemployment and class conflict when railway workers went out on a national strike, joined by miners, mill hands, unemployed workers, women, and children. Socialist radicals seized control of St. Louis and Cincinnati. Hayes restored order by calling out federal troops, an ironic step in that he had withdrawn federal troops in the South, leaving freed slaves at the mercy of whites, who were often willing to use violence through groups such as the Ku Klux Klan to regain political power.

In response to economic depression and the decline in prices, debtors, farmers, and urban workers called for expanding the money supply by issuing paper money called "greenbacks." In 1876 the Greenback Party presidential candidate received more than one million votes and elected fourteen of its candidates to Congress. The Greenbacks declined once the economy rebounded, but many farmers continued to demand inflation through the free and unlimited coinage of silver. Congress responded modestly to these demands, but challenges to a gold-based currency continued to find periodic expression throughout the late nineteenth century.

The tariff and money issues separated Republicans and Democrats. The Republican Party, representing manufacturing interests, called for high tariffs and keeping the gold standard, which allowed the redemption of money in gold. Democrats wanted low tariffs and greenbacks or silver coins. Republican candidates continued to wave the "bloody shirt" by reminding party faithful that the Democrats were the party of rebellion.

In this age of excess, reformers found little influence. Disgusted by corruption, party factionalism, social conflict, and the dominance of party bosses, men and women reformers called for the end of the patronage system and its replacement with a professional civil service based on merit, education, and training. Derided by their opponents as *mugwumps*, an Algonquin Indian word meaning "kingpins," these reformers were elitists who were especially repulsed by the ability of local and state political machines, controlled by party bosses, to march seemingly ignorant voters to the polls to cast ballots for candidates nominated in boss-controlled conventions.

Political machines successfully mobilized their followers on Election Days with turnout rates that often soared to more than 80 percent. Even the dead rose from their graves to vote. Political campaigns became comparable to military campaigns, with martial torchlight parades, excited rallies, and mass street demonstrations. Women and children, even though excluded from voting, were eager participants as the two armies, Republicans and Democrats, confronted one another in political battle. A large number of children were named for political candidates. Only in some localities and states were women granted the right to vote. This led women such as Elizabeth Cady Stanton, Susan B. Anthony, and Lucy Stone to push for a constitutional amendment for women's suffrage. Blacks were allowed to vote in the North, but discriminatory voting laws in the South set up barriers that excluded them from exercising their federal rights. Literacy tests and polls taxes there disenfranchised blacks and poor whites, leading to low voter turnout and class resentment.

Voting tended to break down along ethnic and religious lines. Catholics, Jews, and white Protestants in the South were generally Democratic. Southern blacks who voted remained Republican. In the north, white Protestants of British, Scandinavian, and Dutch ancestry were usually Republicans. Irish Catholics tended to be Democrats. Given that many urban machines were based around local saloons, evangelical Protestant Republicans in the North called for local and state governments to prohibit the sale of liquor—a demand that offended Irish whiskey drinkers and German beer drinkers.

As illustrated in a 1908 magazine cover (see page 78), women were especially active in the prohibition movement through a Woman's Christian Temperance Union led by Frances Willard. Prohibition expressed sentiments in favor of cultural uniformity evident in other campaigns against immigration, Catholics, gambling, and prostitution. Poverty and crime were blamed on alcohol. In these cultural wars, the rise of corporate monopolies and the inordinate influence of special business interests in politics at all levels were overlooked.

Collusion between politicians and business interests created an environment of corruption. Social ills of rapidly growing cities festered. Middle-class reformers, including Chicago social worker Jane Addams, stepped in to introduce community centers and

"What Fools these Mortals be!"

Puck

THE LIPS THAT TOUCH CORN LIKKER SHALL NEVER TOUCH OURN

"MARCHING THROUGH GEORGIA."

5. This 1908 cover of the satiric magazine *Puck* projects an image of female temperance marchers in Georgia as self-righteous, angry, and middle-aged, carrying a banner that reads, "The lips that touch corn likker shall never touch ourn." Women reformers were at the forefront of temperance, suffrage, and peace movements in the late nineteenth century.

social settlement houses in working-class and immigrant neighborhoods. Other reformers promoted better parks, recreation programs, and improved public schools. A few middle-class activists spearheaded reform by crusading against machine bosses such as William Marcy Tweed in New York, but these sporadic attempts at local reform did not challenge national politics.

James A. Garfield, a former Civil War general and college president from Ohio, won the White House in 1880, but by only 39,000 votes of nine million cast. Garfield was assassinated by Charles Guiteau, a disgruntled office seeker and religious fanatic. In reaction to this assassination, Garfield's successor, Chester Arthur, backed a modest measure creating a civil service commission to examine candidates for federal jobs. Yet, even with civil service reform, business interests actually increased their influence in this period. The Senate became known as the Millionaires Club.

The nomination of James Blaine of Maine to head the Republican ticket in 1884 proved to be the final straw for the liberal wing of the party. Blaine had been caught taking a bribe from the Union Pacific Railroad in the "Continental" scandal. The liberal Republican mugwump faction bolted to endorse the Democratic nominee, Grover Cleveland, the reform governor of New York. The 1884 campaign proved especially bitter. Early on, Republicans revealed that Cleveland had fathered an illegitimate child. He immediately admitted the charge, but Republicans continued to chant at Cleveland rallies, "Ma, Ma, where's my pa? Gone to the White House, ha, ha, ha." Democrats shot back, "Blaine, James G. Blaine, the continental liar from the state of Maine." The atmosphere worsened when a leading Protestant minister in Blaine's presence denounced Democrats as the party of "rum, Romanism [Catholicism] and rebellion." The comment enraged some immigrants who had been moving toward Blaine. Cleveland won a narrow victory with a popular vote of a little more than thirty thousand over his opponent. The Prohibition Party won sixteen thousand votes in the critical state of New York, which may have cost Blaine the election.

In the campaign, Cleveland cast himself as a reformer in favor of reducing government activity, balancing the budget, and lowering the tariff. But when he vetoed legislation to extend pensions for Civil War veterans, a program that already accounted for a quarter of the federal budget, veterans turned on him. Cleveland attacked misappropriation of public land sales in the West and refused to support relief for drought-stricken farmers, which drew fire from Western ranchers, Midwest farmers, mine owners, and railroad interests. He reduced tariff rates, a major source of federal revenue, and this alienated entrenched interests. Business interests in general disliked the Interstate Commerce Commission Act in 1887, which created a federal commission to oversee railroad rates.

His reforms earned him the plurality of the popular vote when he came up for reelection, but he lost the Electoral College to the Republican, former U.S. Senator Benjamin Harrison of Indiana. Nobody believed Harrison, the grandson of the former president William Henry Harrison, was a reformer. After the election, Congress went on a massive spending program thus placating special interests. The Billion Dollar Congress, as it became known, doubled the size of the veterans' pension program; expanded the money supply through silver purchases; and enacted a high tariff. One of the few measures toward reform was the enactment of the Sherman Antitrust Act (1890), the first antitrust legislation in the nation's history. This gesture failed to appease public outrage. Democrats swept the midterm elections, but it was already too late to undo the damage. Harrison turned a $3 million budget surplus into a deficit.

Cleveland regained the White House in a landslide victory in 1892, but his reform agenda abruptly halted in 1893 when the nation entered into one of the worse economic depressions in the nation's history. His program of government austerity and hard money did little to ease the suffering of unemployed workers or debt-ridden farmers. The nation was wracked by labor violence and social protest. In early May 1894, thousands of unemployed workers organized into what was called Coxey's Army and marched on Washington demanding a federally sponsored roads project to put people to work. The following summer more violence erupted when the American Railway Union went out on strike in twenty-seven states. The strike was broken when Cleveland ordered in federal troops. Ironically, the strike's leader, Eugene Debs, was arrested and convicted under the Sherman Antitrust Act for entering into a conspiracy to restrain trade. Debs, who had voted for Cleveland, left prison an avowed socialist.

Debt-ridden farmers demanded inflation through coining silver money, which meant creating a bimetallic standard based on gold and silver. Behind this demand lay a strong sentiment against the accumulation of excessive wealth that had come with the rise of corporations. Cleveland's attempt to repeal the Sherman Silver Purchase Act, enacted in 1890 under Harrison, created a firestorm in Congress. Once hailed as a reformer, Cleveland now was portrayed as a tool of Wall Street. A young Populist congressman from Nebraska, William Jennings Bryan, gained national attention in assailing Cleveland's antisilver position. This clash reflected deep fissures within the Democratic Party between those supporting the gold standard ("gold bugs") and Silverites who wanted a bimetallic monetary system.

The call for a bimetallic monetary system was joined by an insurgent farmers' Alliance movement that had sprung up in Texas, and then spread through the South into the Midwest. Even before the depression of 1893, farmer-oriented third parties had elected four governors in the 1890 midterm elections. This movement coalesced into the People's Party, usually called Populists. The Populists articulated agrarian resentment against railroads and banks. The party platform drafted in Omaha demanded the free and unlimited coinage of silver, a graduated income tax, government ownership of telegraph and railroads, and restrictions on immigration. In 1892, the Populists nominated General James Baird Weaver for president. He received more than a million votes, 8.5 percent of the total, and carried six western states. The economic crisis gave Populists hopes for winning the White House in 1896.

When the Democrats met in Chicago in 1896, the silver issue split the party. At the convention, the thirty-six-year-old William Jennings Bryan, now a Democrat, who had carefully set himself up for the presidential nomination, rose to speak on behalf of the pro-silver platform. In a rich, melodic voice he declared, "You shall not crucify mankind upon a cross of gold." He electrified the convention and won the nomination. The Eastern gold wing of the party was left stunned. Populists, for their part, decided to support Bryan, while nominating their own vice-presidential candidate.

Republicans turned to William McKinley from Ohio. He was a solid gold man and supporter of a high tariff. The 1896 presidential race offered two clear, contrasting economic agendas. The race introduced to two new features: money (on the part of Republicans) and a new way of politicking (on the part of Democrats). McKinley's manager, Mark Hanna, a wealthy Cleveland businessman, brought political astuteness not seen since Martin Van Buren to the campaign. Hanna envisioned bringing new urban working-class voters to the Republican's banner and raised unheard-of sums of money playing up fears of Bryan's "radicalism." Republicans received $250,000 from Standard Oil, an amount nearly equal to the entire budget for the Democrats. New York financier J.P. Morgan gave $250,000, while various railroads contributed $174,000. Hanna dispensed nearly $2 million to produce 120 campaign documents and 275 pamphlets, published in dozens of languages. Urban workers in the Northeast and Midwest were warned that Bryan's silver program would prolong the depression. In the end, Republicans spent more than $3.5 million on the campaign. McKinley stayed home in Canton, Ohio, where crowds of voters, eventually totaling 750,000 people, came to hear him give speeches.

Bryan, an evangelist by nature, took his message directly to the voters, traveling 18,000 miles to give six hundred speeches to an estimated million people in twenty-one states. He was the first candidate to make a systematic tour of battleground states since Douglas in 1860. Bryan spoke tirelessly about free silver, declaring that the election was between plutocracy and democracy. He drew huge crowds numbering in the tens of thousands. The size of the crowds worried Republicans, but Mark Hanna reassured them, "He's talking silver all the time and that's where we've got him." He understood that Bryan's radical message frightened voters. Opponents accused Bryan's supporters of being pirates raiding the nation's wealth.

6. William Jennings Bryan, Democratic presidential candidate in 1896, plays a violin on the ship *Popocracy* to lure the "National Prosperity" ship to his crew of pirates, bandits out to raid legitimate wealth. The woman among the pirates is the Populist orator Mary Lease.

The election had the excitement of 1860 all over again. Nearly 95 percent of the voters in some Midwestern states turned out—mostly for McKinley. In the Democratic South, however, turnout fell. McKinley swamped Bryan at the polls, winning six hundred thousand more votes than his Democratic rival, 7.1 million to 6.5 million. Republicans won urban workers and Catholics in the East and Midwest. For the next sixteen years Republicans would control the White House. The first major realignment had occurred in American politics since the 1860 election. Democrats had swallowed the Populists, but radicalism had turned many conservative Democrats into Republicans.

McKinley had been elected on domestic issues, but foreign policy, particularly Cuba's struggle to gain independence from Spain, quickly absorbed his first term. The depression of 1893 led many within his party to become imperialist in pressing for new export markets and colonies. The ideology of Social Darwinism—a view that society was dominated by competition between individuals, groups, and nations—reinforced this call for economic expansion. Reports of Spanish atrocities published by competing newspapers added to the cry for war, which finally came in 1898. In this "splendid little war," as Secretary of State John Hay called it, a defeated Spain relinquished control of Cuba and Puerto Rico, as well as the Philippine Islands in the Pacific. Cuba became independent, but under strong American influence. McKinley's proposal to annex the Philippines in the midst of a Filipino insurrection led opponents to form the Anti-Imperialist League.

McKinley's assassination shortly after his reelection brought Vice President Theodore Roosevelt to the White House in 1901. He had been placed on the ticket because he was from New York and was a Spanish-American War hero. A Republican maverick, he made corporate monopoly a primary focus of his presidency, ushering in a period of progressive reform that lasted until America's entry into the First World War in 1917.

Reform became a moral crusade. Progressive reformers divided over issues such as Prohibition, narcotics control, and immigration, but they agreed that politics needed to be cleaned up. Progressive reform had begun on the local level and moved through the states. Demands for more active government came from trade associations, professional groups, consumer leagues, women activists, and labor unions. Reformers on the local and state levels called for efficiency and economy in government and introduced party primaries, ballot initiatives, and referenda to empower voters. Cities and states became hotbeds for experiments in reform. In New York City, Seth Low, elected mayor in 1902, introduced a civil service system for municipal employees aimed at cleaning up graft. In Toledo, Ohio, reform mayor Samuel Jones opened free kindergartens, developed a park system, instituted an eight-hour day for city workers, and took away truncheons from the police. City reform movements appeared in Philadelphia, Detroit, Baltimore, Cincinnati, Seattle, San Francisco, Los Angeles, and other cities.

Oregon, Wisconsin, and California became experiments in democratic reform. Oregon reformer William U'Ren put together a coalition of farmers, unions, and middle-class citizens to successfully promote in his state a presidential primary system, direct election of U.S. senators, and direct democracy through initiatives, referendums, and recalls of elected officials. In Wisconsin progressive Republicans, led by Governor Robert LaFollette, passed laws regulating factory safety, established a state income tax, limited working hours for women and children, and passed forest and waterpower conservation acts. In California progressives elected Hiram Johnson, who called for throwing corporate interests out of politics.

In his presidency (1901–09), Theodore Roosevelt promoted antitrust prosecution, consumer protection, and environmental conservation. He believed the federal government should serve as an arbitrator between labor and capital, and not serve one interest over the other. He demanded that corporate trusts that had illegally driven rivals out of business should be prosecuted under antitrust laws by the Department of Justice. In pursuing his agenda, he strengthened the office of the presidency. His vigorous leadership during a national coal strike in 1902 showed that government could be a neutral voice in labor conflict. In 1906, in response to public demand caused by socialist Upton Sinclair's muckraking novel *The Jungle*, Roosevelt pushed through Congress the Meat Inspection Act. This was followed the same year with the Pure Food and Drug Act establishing the Food and Drug Administration. Working with Gifford Pinchot, a wealthy Pennsylvania environmentalist, Roosevelt secured major conservation legislation and established five new national parks: Crater Lake, Oregon; Wind Cave, South Dakota; Sully's Hill, North Dakota (now a game preserve); Mesa Verde, Colorado; and Platt, Oklahoma (now a national recreation area).

Roosevelt, who had won a full term on his own, campaigning for a "square deal" in 1904, left the presidency immensely popular. He was able to pass on the reform banner to his handpicked successor, William Howard Taft, who easily won the presidency against William Jennings Bryan in 1908.

Roosevelt believed Taft shared his progressive outlook, but temperamentally Taft was cautious and legalistic. Weighing more than three hundred pounds, he cut a much different figure than the athletic Roosevelt, who had literally charged up San Juan Hill in Cuba during the Spanish-American War. Taft underestimated the emotion of the reform movement sweeping across America. Although his administration undertook more antitrust prosecutions than Roosevelt's had, he was seen by many within the Republican Party, especially Senator LaFollette, former Wisconsin governor, as being a tool of Wall Street. He extended Interstate Commerce Commission control over the telephone and telegraph industry, but this was not enough to satisfy his critics. His bungling of tariff reform further alienated progressives in his party.

As a result, Republicans entered the 1912 presidential election divided once again. Offended by Taft's betrayal, Roosevelt challenged him for the Republican nomination. But after winning most primaries, Roosevelt failed to win the nomination when Taft used presidential patronage to secure delegates in the South and nonprimary states. Roosevelt supporters stormed out of the convention to form the Progressive Party. At their convention they sang the old religious gospel song "Onward Christian Soldiers," nominated Theodore Roosevelt, and pledged to enact a minimum wage for female workers, child labor legislation, social security insurance, women's suffrage, and national health insurance (which had been endorsed earlier by the American Medical Association). Roosevelt knew that his move would split the party, but he was determined to see Taft lose, even if a Democrat won.

Democrats felt reform in the air. They nominated Woodrow Wilson, a Virginia-born history professor, former president of Princeton University, and recently elected governor of New Jersey. Because of the rule that a candidate needed two-thirds of the delegates, Wilson's selection came after the forty-sixth ballot, when William Jennings Bryan threw his support to Wilson.

In 1912, Americans demanded an activist federal government. They wanted, if necessary, a more interventionist government willing to undertake more coercive action to regulate corporate abuses and reform government at all levels from special interest influence. Taft, Roosevelt, and Wilson all declared themselves progressives. A fourth candidate, Eugene Debs, running as the Socialist Party nominee on a platform to nationalize basic industries, gave further evidence of the electorate's sentiment for government activism. Taft was left defending the status quo, and the contest came down to Roosevelt and Wilson. Both addressed the issue of regulating the large corporations that had transformed the American economy. Roosevelt called for a "New Nationalism" that distinguished "good" corporations from "bad" trusts manipulating the marketplace. Wilson, drawing on the advice of a young Boston lawyer, Louis

Brandeis, called for a "New Freedom" to break up large business and restore the competitive market economy.

Wilson won because Republicans split their vote. While only gaining 42 percent of the popular vote, he carried forty-one of the forty-eight states. Wilson received about six million votes, Roosevelt four million, and Taft three million. Roosevelt became the only third party candidate to come in second. Remarkably, Debs got nearly nine hundred thousand votes. For the first time since the Civil War, a southern Democrat entered the White House. Observers noted that Wilson's meteoric rise in politics compared to Jackson's insurgency in 1824.

His administration marked the triumph of progressive reform. Supported by progressive majorities in Congress, Wilson in his first term signed legislation reducing the tariff, enacting a new income tax (enabled by the ratification of the Sixteenth Amendment in 1913), and created the Federal Trade Commission to regulate industry. The establishment of a centralized banking system through the Federal Reserve Act of 1913 marked his greatest achievement, although critics saw the central bank as favoring big banking. His achievements were marred by his support of his postmaster general in segregating black and white employees.

Wilson won reelection in 1916 by promising to keep America out of the world war that had broken out in Europe in 1914. His neutrality pledge proved untenable when German U-boats (submarines) attacked American shipping. On April 2, 1917, Wilson received from Congress a declaration of war against Germany. The resolution to "make the world safe for democracy" passed the Senate by a vote of 82 to 6, and the House by 375 to 50.

As patriotic fever swept the nation, and a national draft system was enacted, socialists, labor radicals, and pacifists denounced the war. On the local and state level, patriotic organizations emerged to attack antiwar opponents, sometimes violently. Congress enacted the Espionage and Sedition Acts to make it unlawful to criticize the government or war policies, and people went to prison under the acts. (The Espionage Act remained in force into the twenty-first century.) When the war ended in 1918, many Americans had become disillusioned with Wilson. Progressive reform had achieved much, but its consequence, the rise of big government, became the focus for political debate extending into the twenty-first century.

Chapter 7
Affluence, depression, and world war, 1920–45

The quarter-century from 1920 to 1945 proved to be both critical and transformative for American government. Americans witnessed in these twenty-five years an economic boom in the 1920s, a global depression beginning in 1929 that led to the creation of the modern welfare state and the realignment of the two parties, and winning a terrible global war in the 1940s that threatened Western democracies.

Although the progressive impulse for the most part abated in the 1920s, the Great Depression of the 1930s revived reform under the presidency of Franklin Roosevelt (1933–45). Under his administration, the federal government extended its involvement in the economy, its regulatory powers in banking, consumer affairs, and labor relations, and established welfare programs through the Social Security Act (1935). At the same time, the adjudicatory role of government was extended through the establishment of new agencies such as the National Labor Relations Board. A realignment of voters provided the opportunity for the Democratic Party to form a new political coalition composed of organized labor, northern ethnic voters, blacks, and white southerners. In control of the White House and Congress throughout the 1930s, Democrats passed major legislation that established the modern welfare and regulatory state. Republicans fought a rear-guard action against what they perceived to be the excesses of big government, erosion of federalism, and threats to individual liberty. Southern Democrats, while welcoming much of the New Deal, were particularly adamant in support of "states rights," then a code word for maintaining racial segregation in the South.

World War One ended in disillusionment for the American people. Wilson had suppressed dissent at home and extended control to a wide range of industries including railroads, steel, and shipping. During the war, the government prosecuted close to 1,500 war dissenters, including sending socialist Eugene Debs to federal prison for sedition.

The last gasps of progressivism came with the ratification of the Eighteenth and Nineteenth Amendments to the Constitution in 1920, allowing Congress to prohibit the sale of alcoholic beverages and giving women suffrage rights, respectively. After ratification of the amendment prohibiting the sale of alcohol, Congress passed the Volstead Act, over Wilson's veto, to stiffen Prohibition. The Nineteenth Amendment marked the triumph of a long campaign. In this struggle, towns, counties, states, and territories, such as Wyoming and Utah, emerged as laboratories of democracy by giving women voting rights. In 1917, Alice Paul and Lucy Burns formed the National Woman's Party that provided impetus for the final ratification of the Nineteenth Amendment.

Wilson sought an even greater goal: establishing the League of Nations to end all wars. In 1919, he attended the Paris Peace Conference to secure this. Relations with Republicans in Congress were strained by his vigorous and unsuccessful campaign the year before to keep a Democrat-controlled Congress. Upon his return from Paris, where he had won European support for the new league, Wilson confronted a hostile Republican leadership in the Senate led by Henry Cabot Lodge, chairman of the Foreign Relations Committee. Lodge held up ratification of the treaty that established the league; in November 1919 and again in March

1920 the Senate voted against it. So the president decided to take his case directly to the American people through an extensive speaking tour. While on tour in October 1919, he experienced physical exhaustion and returned to Washington where he suffered a stroke. As government drifted, his wife, Edith, managed most of Wilson's affairs.

The recovering Wilson decided to make the league the focus of the Democratic Party's 1920 campaign. Voters, however, were concerned with other issues. Consumer prices had jumped in 1919, and labor discontent swept the nation. In February 1919, more than sixty thousand union workers went on strike in Seattle. In September, the police walked out in Boston. After two days of rioting, Massachusetts governor Calvin Coolidge called out the National Guard, declaring that there was no right to strike against public safety. That same month six hundred thousand steel workers struck. Fears of a communist conspiracy grew following the Bolshevik revolution in the Soviet Union in 1917 and labor upheavals of 1919 in the United States. In response, U.S. Attorney General A. Mitchell Palmer, a presidential hopeful, directed underling J. Edgar Hoover to round up thousands of alleged foreign-born radicals, 249 of whom were later deported to the Soviet Union, now under Communist control. Race riots broke out in fifteen cities, including Chicago, which cost the lives of twenty-three blacks and fifteen whites. (Race riots in 1919 usually meant vigilante whites attacking blacks.)

While Wilson and the Democrats sought to make the presidential election of 1920 about the league, Republicans talked about a return to "normalcy," but they lacked a clear favorite to head the ticket. The Chicago convention deadlocked. In a closed meeting party leaders picked Senator Warren G. Harding of Ohio. It took another nine votes on the convention floor to finally secure his nomination. Calvin Coolidge was nominated for vice president. Republicans called for lower taxes and smaller government. They condemned Democratic candidate James Cox and his running mate, Franklin Roosevelt, a distant relative of Theodore, for their support of "Wilson's League." Harding pursued McKinley's strategy of staying at home, leaving campaign travel to Coolidge. In a landslide Republicans took the White House, the Senate, and the House. For the first time, women in every state were able to vote, but only about 50 percent of the eligible voters went to the polls, a pattern that lasted for the rest of the century. Women, though, became active in civic organizations devoted to peace, consumer affairs, labor rights, and child welfare. In 1920 Congress established the Women's Bureau, an agency in the Labor Department exclusively devoted to female workers.

Republican presidents of the 1920s produced a mixed record. Harding pardoned the imprisoned Eugene Debs, appointed a record number of women to his administration, and urged the passage a federal antilynching law, although he refused to use the federal government to stop the terrorism of a nationally revived Ku Klux Klan. Secretary of the Treasury Andrew Mellon pursued pro-business policies built around high tariffs and tax reductions. The administration expanded federal power by increasing federal subsidies for the fledgling airline industry and federal aid for highway construction. The first national budget system was created. Harding's successors Coolidge and Hoover undertook reforms of the Indian Bureau and prisons while he expanded agricultural and medical education for blacks. His administration extended federal regulation of coastal waters and radio.

Republican presidents, however, would be remembered most for scandal and depression. Corruption overwhelmed Harding's administration. When the assistant to Attorney General Harry Daughtery committed suicide, investigators found that Daughtery had allowed the Justice Department to sell hundreds of pardons to bootleggers and tax evaders. More revelations followed: the director of the Veterans Bureau was indicted for embezzling $200 million. Secretary of Interior Albert Fall received payoffs in the form of low-interest loans from oil executives to secure leases of federal lands in California and Teapot Dome, Wyoming. These scandals were just breaking when Harding suffered a heart attack and died in July 1923. Following his death, further revelations came of his gambling and extramarital affairs.

Notably reserved, Calvin Coolidge brought a calm reassurance to the nation. He pushed further tax reductions for high-income earners, eventually reducing the highest marginal rate to 40 percent. By 1927, 98 percent of the population paid no income tax. Mostly due to his reductions in the costs of government, the national debt fell from $22.3 billion in 1923 to $16 billion in 1929.

He pushed out rivals to win the Republican nomination in 1924. Behind his back experienced politicians joked that Coolidge "got his first base on balls [Massachusetts governorship], stole around second base [Boston police strike] to third [vice president] on an error and reached home because the catcher fell dead." In 1924, a small group of progressives within the party broke to back Robert LaFollette, who accepted the nomination of the Progressive Party. At the divisive Democratic convention an active Ku Klux Klan blocked Governor Al Smith of New York, a Roman Catholic, from the nomination. After an unprecedented 103 ballots, the party finally turned to Wall Street lawyer John W. Davis. The incumbent President Coolidge had prosperity going for him and two weak opponents; he garnered more votes than both of his rival candidates combined.

Tapping into xenophobic fears of cultural erosion and organized labor's concerns with cheap immigrant labor, Congress passed the National Origins Act in 1924, which placed a quota on immigrants coming from southern and eastern Europe, while allowing unlimited immigration from the Western Hemisphere and the Philippines. A proviso excluded Japanese immigration. The act passed by sweeping bipartisan majorities in both houses.

Economic prosperity set the stage for Herbert Hoover's nomination by the Republican Party in 1928, when Coolidge decided not to seek reelection. Hoover campaigned on "A chicken in every pot, and a car in every garage." After the disaster of 1924, Democrats turned finally to Al Smith, a reform-minded candidate who understood the problems of an increasingly urbanized country. Smith was the first Catholic to win nomination by a major party. While Hoover kept religion out of the campaign, others did not. Reverend Bob Jones Sr., a leading Protestant evangelical preacher, delivered more than a thousand speeches opposing a Catholic in the White House. In fairness, mudslinging was not one-sided. Democrats accused Hoover of being a British citizen because he owned two houses in England. Nonetheless, on Election Day, 58 percent of the popular vote and 444 electoral votes went to Hoover. The only good news for Democrats was that Smith received 6.6 million more votes than the Democrats had polled four years earlier. He pulled in many first-time Catholic voters in the urban Northeast, and the big cities started to vote Democratic.

Hoover stepped into the White House wildly popular among the voters, although not well liked by regulars in his party who saw him as too progressive. Orphaned at an early age, Hoover became a multimillionaire as a mining and hydroelectric dam engineer. He gave up his comfortable life to devote himself to public service, serving under Wilson in World War One as head of the Food Administration and under Harding and Coolidge as Secretary of Commerce. He was to leave the White House four years later as one of the most unpopular presidents in history.

Hoover lacked the political skills or temperament to be a successful president in the worse depression in American history, which began with a crash on Wall Street in October 1929. Prior to entering the White House, Hoover had called economic speculation on Wall Street "crazy and dangerous." By 1930, the administration acknowledged that 4.5 million Americans were out of work. Hoover worked himself to the point of near exhaustion in trying to rally Americans and businesses caught in this precipitate economic downturn. He proposed a massive public works program, only to have Democrats in Congress defeat his proposal because they felt it did not go far enough. With government expenditures only 2.5 percent of the economy, he worried about rising budget deficits. Finally, an energized Congress did accept his proposal for a Reconstruction Finance Corporation to provide relief to failing banks and financial institutions. And Congress enacted the Glass-Steagall Act (1932) extending Federal Reserve powers over banking. A Federal Home Loan Bank Act was enacted to stimulate home construction. It was not enough to revive an economy in free fall.

In 1932, Republicans nominated Hoover for a second term knowing that it was a lost cause. A faction-ridden Democratic National Convention picked Franklin Roosevelt, the fifty-year-old reform governor of New York. Roosevelt called for "bold, persistent experimentation" to address the nation's ills. His charming personality, his self-assuredness, and his innate optimism captured the imagination of the American public. His own struggle to overcome polio contracted in 1921 at the age of thirty-one, which left him paralyzed from the waist down, imparted inspiration to a public caught in an economy that itself seemed paralyzed. On the campaign trail, Roosevelt remained vague on many issues, attacking Hoover as a spendthrift, even while calling for bold governmental action. In the midst of the presidential campaign in the summer of 1932, Hoover ordered federal troops under General Douglas MacArthur to forcibly disband about twenty thousand World War One veterans camped in Washington demanding prepayment of a veterans' bonus. The public backlash against this action cemented Hoover's image as a man removed from the people. On November 8, 1932, forty-two of the forty-eight states voted for Roosevelt. Only 40 percent of the voters opted for Hoover. Democrats swept Congress, giving Roosevelt a mandate for change.

Roosevelt brought to his presidency a willingness to experiment amidst the worst economic downturn in American history. Scholars of the Great Depression continue to debate the economic effectiveness of New Deal programs and whether Roosevelt's policies prolonged it. The myriad programs, labor militancy, and Roosevelt's attacks on big business as "economic royalists" unsettled businessmen already confronting unfavorable market conditions. Critics, then and now, could not deny that Roosevelt was the most adroit politician of the twentieth century. His building of a New Deal coalition of the industrial northeast, the South, organized labor, blacks, Catholics, and Jews realigned the parties and dominated American politics for the next half-century. Republicans would not win the White House again until November 1952, and only then because they nominated a war hero, Dwight D. Eisenhower.

As governor of New York, Roosevelt experimented with new programs to cope with the stock market crash, including a massive state public works program. His experience as governor reinforced his experimental temperament, which he brought to his presidency. He immediately confronted a major crisis with the collapse of the entire banking system just prior to his inauguration. In addition, the welfare and relief system, based on a preindustrial order of local voluntarism and modest state involvement, broke under the strain of massive unemployment. Gathering around him a group of professors, mostly from Columbia University, known as the Brains Trust, Roosevelt brought before Congress new legislation to address the emergency.

Over the course of the next hundred days, the Democratic Congress passed legislation, often without reading the bills, restoring banks, repealing Prohibition, establishing the National Recovery Administration to fix prices and wages, and allowing the Department of Agriculture to subsidize farmers not to grow crops. Congress established the Securities and Exchange Commission to oversee Wall Street. A new home loan act passed. Congress

DEPRESSION

7. A 1934 photograph captures the demoralization of the unemployed in the Great Depression, which FDR's New Deal sought to overcome.

enacted legislation creating massive public works projects. Using his presidential power, Roosevelt took the country off the domestic gold standard. For a brief time, the economy rebounded, and then it fell back into depression.

The public saw that Roosevelt was an activist and experimenter. They approved, and in the midterm elections of 1934 Democrats made further gains in Congress and state legislatures.

The continuation of the depression, however, fostered Roosevelt's opponents on the left and the right. In 1934, socialist Upton Sinclair won the Democratic nomination for the California governorship. Roosevelt discreetly refused to endorse him in what turned out to be a losing campaign. Roosevelt found himself under attack from other quarters. In Detroit popular radio priest Charles Coughlin, a believer in free silver, attacked Roosevelt's

"Jew Deal." In California retired dentist Francis Townsend criticized the New Deal for not doing enough for the elderly and organized a grassroots movement calling for a pension system for them. In Louisiana U.S. Senator Huey Long attacked Roosevelt from the left by organizing a national movement called "Share Our Wealth" to "soak the rich" by redistributing wealth and giving every American a federal guaranteed income of $200 a month. The small Communist Party turned to organizing popular fronts with liberal groups. Communism appealed mostly to a small group of intellectuals and writers with some influence on the cultural front, but also attracted some labor organizers in the American Federation of Labor and the newly formed Congress of Industrial Organizations (CIO).

Roosevelt responded with audacity. The administration established the Works Progress Administration, headed by New York social worker Harry Hopkins, to undertake new construction projects and establish programs to support unemployed writers and artists. In 1935, Roosevelt signed the most important piece of legislation of his administration, establishing Social Security. Although limited in its coverage and intended only as a supplement to private pensions, the act provided aid to the elderly, indigent, and single women (mostly widows at the time). The same bill established unemployment insurance and workmen's compensation programs through federal-state arrangements.

Roosevelt's popularity and New Deal programs placed Republicans completely on the defensive. They could not decide on whether to denounce the New Deal as socialist or to go along with it. In 1935 conservative business opposition established the Liberty League, financed by members of the du Pont family and other corporate leaders. Former Roosevelt allies Al Smith and John J. Raskob became members. The league became an easy foil for Roosevelt, who played upon class sentiment to attack his opponents. Opposition to his right played into the already popular president's hands. From the left came Huey Long, Charles Coughlin, and Francis Townsend who joined together to form a third party. However, Long's assassination in September 1935 put an end to that threat. In 1936 the Union Party nominated North Dakota congressman William Lemke, who received 2 percent of the national vote.

Republicans turned to Alf Landon, the governor of Kansas, to head the ticket. He had been one of the few Republicans to win in 1934. Republicans raised about $11.6 million to oust Roosevelt, compared with $8.3 million by the Democrats. Organized labor cemented its ties to the Democrats by spending almost $800,000 during the campaign. Roosevelt swept every state except Vermont and Maine, winning 60 percent of the popular vote and all but eight electoral votes. Democrats increased their totals in both houses of Congress and state governorships. The election revealed sharp polarization along class lines. Upper-income groups went overwhelmingly Republican, while lower-income groups voted Democratic. Unfortunately for Republicans in 1936, there were more poor than wealthy in America. One consequence of the election for the Republicans was that power shifted to the moderate eastern wing of the party.

New Deal programs helped foster a popular democratic culture. The Works Progress Administration hired artists to decorate post offices with murals, actors performed free plays in parks, and writers turned out tourist books and state histories. Hollywood promoted popular democracy in such films as *Mr. Smith Goes to Washington* (1939). This democratic ethos spurred blacks, Hispanics, women, and workers to organize within their communities and nationally. Democratic sentiment found expression in the drive to organize industrial workers in the Congress of Industrial Organizations, formed in 1935.

For a gambler or a politician, hubris often leads to a downfall. Convinced of his mandate, Roosevelt proposed the Judicial

Reorganization Act to allow him to expand membership on the Supreme Court with six new appointees. Frustrated by court decisions that had ruled key New Deal legislation unconstitutional, including the National Industrial Recovery Act, the Agricultural Adjustment Act, and minimum wages for female workers, Roosevelt reacted with a vengeance. Republicans said little, letting a public and media backlash force leading Democrats to attack the "court packing scheme," which was ultimately buried by the Senate.

A few days before Roosevelt announced his Supreme Court legislation, labor violence broke out in Flint, Michigan, instigated by company agents, when the United Auto Workers began a sit-down strike at a General Motors (GM) plant. Roosevelt purposely took a neutral stance, which alienated labor leaders including John L. Lewis of the Congress for Industrial Workers. GM eventually settled the strike in favor of organized labor, which now emerged as a major force in the Democratic Party.

In the midst of these troubles, the economy fell into recession in September 1937. This drop was more severe than the crash of 1929. Roosevelt turned to young economists influenced by John Maynard Keynes, who urged a deliberate policy of deficit spending. Roosevelt proposed $4.5 billion for public housing, highway construction, and farm subsidies. The Fair Labor Standards Act (1938) set minimum wages and maximum hours for workers. Roosevelt openly targeted big business by investigating monopolies, regulating transportation, and imposing new corporate taxes and higher income tax rates on upper-income groups.

In the 1938 midterm elections, Roosevelt decided to purge his opponents in the Democratic Party by directly intervening in primaries. He targeted five senators, and in each case failed. After 1938 Roosevelt confronted a Congress dominated by a conservative coalition of Republicans and Southern Democrats that would prevail for decades.

The outbreak of World War Two in Europe in September 1939 transformed political debate in America. Although they disliked Nazi Germany, most Americans were reluctant to get directly involved in another world war. When Roosevelt asked Congress to replace an arms embargo against warring nations with a cash-and-carry policy to aid Britain, thousands of telegrams flooded Congress pleading to "keep America out of the blood business." Isolationists in Congress and in organizations such as the America First Committee attacked the president's interventionist policies. To ensure bipartisan support for his program of preparing the nation for war, Roosevelt in 1940 appointed two Republicans to his cabinet.

Those appointments stole thunder from Republicans on the eve of their national convention, which took place just as France fell to Hitler. They were dismayed when Roosevelt decided to seek reelection for an unprecedented third term. Polls were in their infancy, but they showed he was the only Democrat who could win. He selected as his running mate liberal New Dealer Henry Wallace, a former Theodore Roosevelt Progressive Republican who left his post as secretary of Agriculture to join the ticket. Isolationist sentiment had been particularly strong among Midwest Republicans, but given the dire situation in Europe, the party turned to internationalist Wendell Willkie, president of the Commonwealth and Southern Utilities Corporation, to head their presidential ticket. Willkie disagreed with Roosevelt's antibusiness policies. Republicans charged Roosevelt with seeking a dictatorship by running for a third term, which was the main campaign issue, but the popular Roosevelt prevailed with a five million vote margin, much less than his eleven million margin in 1936. He especially lost votes in Midwest communities with many of Irish and German ancestry who disliked the idea of the United States going to war to save Britain.

The Japanese attack on Pearl Harbor, Hawaii, on December 7, 1941, and America's subsequent entry into World War Two killed isolationism. Republicans and Democrats rallied to defend the nation. Roosevelt declared that "Dr. New Deal" had been replaced by "Dr. Win-the-War." Yet, partisanship, while subdued, was not dead. In Congress, Republicans sniped at price and wage controls, tax increases, and government bureaucrats. In the 1942 midterm elections, marked by a low turnout, Republicans picked up forty-four seats in the House (thirteen short of the Democrats) and seven in the Senate. Key New Deal agencies were dismantled, and existing agencies involved in postwar domestic planning came under continued attack. Roosevelt pressed forward, calling in 1944 for "a second Bill of Rights" to ensure decent housing, education, jobs, and welfare for Americans.

In the 1944 presidential campaign, Roosevelt, intent on keeping his Southern base, kept away from civil rights. While he appointed hundreds of blacks to posts in his administration, he refused to endorse an antilynching law. The 1944 Democratic platform called for a constitutional amendment guaranteeing equal rights for women, while offering platitudes for black Americans. To placate conservatives in the party who saw that the president was failing physically, Roosevelt agreed to replace Vice President Henry Wallace with Senator Harry S. Truman of Missouri, a liberal with Confederate ancestors who had exposed wartime corruption among defense contractors.

Republicans decided to sell themselves as the party of reform—reform through controlling runaway wartime bureaucracy in Washington. Polls showed that Americans were more concerned about domestic issues than international affairs, even in the midst of a world war. The 1944 Republican platform denounced poll taxes, opposed lynching, called for a permanent civil rights commission, and considered integrating the armed forces. The party nominated Governor Thomas Dewey of New York, who had made his reputation prosecuting organized crime in New York City. Democrats took advantage of close ties to organized labor to help launch large-scale voter registration drives in key industrial states.

Americans did not want to change leaders during the war, and Roosevelt won. Still Republicans felt that Dewey had done surprisingly well against a popular wartime president. In April 1945, just as the war was drawing to a close, Roosevelt died of a cerebral hemorrhage. His inexperienced vice president, Truman, stepped into the White House confronted with a nation still at war and a nation in shock over the president's death. Roosevelt had led the nation through depression and war and transformed politics as no other president in modern America.

One month after taking office, Truman declared victory in Europe and turned his attention to the Pacific war against imperial Japan. Truman, who learned only after he became president of the existence of the development by American scientists of the atomic bomb, decided to use this weapon to end the war quickly. In August 1945, he ordered atomic bombs to be dropped on the Japanese cities of Hiroshima and Nagasaki, which forced the surrender of Japan. Truman now faced the problems of a postwar world, international rivalry with the Soviet Union, anticolonialism in developing nations, and nuclear weapons, which threatened all humankind.

Chapter 8
Early Cold War politics, 1945–74

Cold War rivalry between nuclear powers—the United States and the Soviet Union—set the tone and substance of American politics from the end of the Second World War to the collapse of the Soviet Union in the 1990s. The Cold War dictated nearly every aspect of American politics. Bipartisan foreign policy prevailed until the Vietnam War in the 1960s, but this did not carry over to elections, domestic issues, or day-to-day politics.

Hand-to-hand political combat was conducted increasingly through television, which inevitably increased the cost of campaigns. Along with television, the other most significant change in American politics came with the struggle to overcome racial segregation and to assure equal voting rights for blacks. One of the ironies of this expanded electorate was that on average only about half of the electorate bothered to vote in presidential elections, a continuation of a trend that began at the turn of the twentieth century. The rise of consumer culture in place of mass political culture, voter apathy, and arguably voting restrictions decreased voter turnout. At the same time, the presidency gained more power in the midst of the Cold War, military interventions in foreign countries, and the continued expansion of the regulatory and welfare state.

The New Deal Democratic political coalition remained in place until the 1960s. It was an uneasy alliance of Northern urban machines, organized labor, Southern courthouse rings, and volunteer activist organizations throughout the nation. These Democrats often had different views about national domestic issues, but they were held together by Cold War unity, party control of Congress, and patronage. Democrats tapped into general public support for welfare programs. Republicans relied on anti-New Deal ideology to motivate party faithful, but did not challenge overturning the entire welfare state. Indeed, Republicans supported its incremental growth.

Many liberals such as Secretary of Commerce Henry Wallace hoped to continue the wartime alliance of the Big Three—United States, Great Britain, and the Soviet Union. The willful disregard by Joseph Stalin, leader of the Soviet Union, of the agreements reached at Yalta in 1945 by Roosevelt, British Prime Minister Winston Churchill, and Stalin had increased tensions within the alliance even before Roosevelt's death. As hostilities intensified, profound fears grew of communist subversion at home. The Communist Party, although small in membership, had gained influence during the Second World War in some unions and liberal groups. The discovery of Soviet spy rings in government encouraged a "Red Scare." Grassroots anticommunist crusaders launched hunts for suspected communists while organizing patriotic activities in their communities. Anticommunist themes were found in movies, television programs, pulp books, and even comic books. On the Sabbath, Jews and Christians continued to hear anticommunist messages. At the same time, anticommunist liberals undertook their own campaign to root out communist involvement in unions, civic groups, and political organizations.

After fourteen years of Democratic control of the White House and Congress, Republicans took control of Congress in the 1946 midterm election, gaining fifty-five House seats and twelve Senate seats. Democrats fared well only in the South. Republican candidates, such as Richard Nixon running for Congress in Southern California, took advantage of popular anticommunist sentiment to win the election. Republicans saw the advantages of an anticommunist crusade that targeted liberal groups once tied to communists.

After Republicans won control of Congress, the House Un-American Activities Committee (HUAC) opened hearings into communist influence in Hollywood, universities, labor unions, industry, and government. Under increasing pressure in March 1947, Truman ordered the FBI to investigate all federal employees. In this probe more than three hundred employees resigned—some for personal reasons such as homosexuality, which they did not want revealed publicly by their supervisors. For those questioned by the FBI or HUAC, the only way to prove their loyalty was to "name names" of others involved in communist activities. Senator Joseph McCarthy, a Wisconsin Republican, exploited anticommunist fears, heightened by the outbreak of war in Korea in 1950. His bellicose style and wild charges led Truman to call these tactics McCarthyism, a name that stuck in describing this period. While using the communist issue, Republicans tapped into widespread postwar discontent over housing shortages, wage-price controls, and scandals in the Truman administration.

The Republican-controlled 80th Congress pushed through tax cuts, a balanced budget, a constitutional amendment establishing a two-term limit for presidents, and the controversial Taft-Hartley Act. Southern and western lawmakers supported the law to lure businesses to their regions. Organized labor railed against the bill, which curtailed union activities and allowed states to enact "right-to-work" legislation banning compulsory union membership. Most southern states did so to attract northern factory jobs. Truman vetoed the legislation, only to have Congress override his veto. That veto cemented his support from organized labor.

In 1948 Republicans again nominated Thomas Dewey. To prove his liberalism and win black votes, Truman delivered to Congress

in February 1948 new civil rights legislation, which many
southern Democrats opposed. At the Democratic National
Convention, Hubert Humphrey, the mayor of Minneapolis,
successfully pushed through a plank supporting human rights for
racial minorities. In response, Mississippi and Alabama delegates
bolted the convention to form the States' Rights Party. Labeled the
Dixiecrats, the party nominated Governor Strom Thurmond of
South Carolina for president. After the Dixiecrats walked out,
Truman signed executive orders integrating the armed forces
and federal bureaucracy.

At the same time, Truman faced a threat on his left when Henry
Wallace accepted the nomination of the Progressive Party. Wallace
called for cooperation with the Soviet Union and denounced
Truman's aggressive foreign policy. Wallace's campaign failed
to gain political traction in the larger electorate.

Seeking to place his opponents on the defense, Truman called a
special session of Congress, inviting Republicans to try to pass
their agenda. When Congress enacted no new legislation, Truman
labeled them "the do-nothing, good-for-nothing" Congress. He
pursued a vigorous slashing campaign warning that Dewey
represented the same forces that led to the Great Depression and
fascism in Germany. Crowds turning out at stops along his
30,000-mile railway speaking tour responded, "Give 'em hell,
Harry." Dewey, convinced by the polls that the election was his,
played it safe by not attacking Truman. He was stiff, dull, and
banal on the campaign trail. He also appeared arrogant when
he announced the names of his cabinet before Election Day.

Truman won a stunning upset, getting 303 electoral votes to
Dewey's 189. Truman's support for civil rights rallied 77 percent of
blacks. In a low turnout election, unions helped Democrats at the
polls. Republicans also lost Congress. Thurmond's Dixiecrats
captured four southern states, in all of which Thurmond was
listed as the Democratic candidate. Voters gave Wallace only a

million and half votes, although his tally in New York tipped the state to Dewey.

This victory should have provided a mandate to achieve Truman's promise of a "Fair Deal." His program centered on comprehensive national health insurance and a massive employment program through public works. Both measures failed to gain support in the conservative-dominated Congress. A series of scandals involving corruption within the administration added to Truman's second-term woes. A stalemated war in Korea (1950–53) grew increasingly unpopular. On the whole, Truman's call for a Fair Deal resulted, in the end, in a small deal.

Having lost five presidential elections in a row, Republicans believed that 1952 provided them with an excellent chance to win. Midwestern conservatives, although still tainted with charges of prewar isolationism, fervently believed that Republicans had lost by trying to imitate the New Deal with Willkie and Dewey. They rallied to Senator Robert Taft of Ohio, "Mr. Republican." Their hopes were dashed when Dwight D. Eisenhower, former commander of the Allied invasion of Europe during World War Two, declared his candidacy.

After Eisenhower and Taft went toe to toe in the primaries, Eisenhower supporters won the nomination for their candidate at the convention when disputed Taft delegates from Texas, Georgia, and Louisiana were not seated. To both appease the conservative wing of the party and to provide regional balance, Eisenhower selected as his running mate Senator Richard Nixon of California. Nixon had gained a national reputation for heading the congressional investigation of alleged Soviet agent Alger Hiss, a former high-ranking State Department official.

Democrats turned to the eloquent Governor Adlai Stevenson of Illinois. The Korean War, revelations of corruption in Truman's administration, and grassroots anticommunism hindered him.

Exploiting Eisenhower's magnetic personality, Republicans won with "I like Ike." The Eisenhower-Nixon ticket swept the nation with 55 percent of the popular vote, giving Republicans 442 electoral votes to a meager 89 for Stevenson, who failed even to carry his home state. Republicans carried four Southern states, Virginia, Tennessee, Florida, and Texas, the sixth most populous state in the country. Eisenhower's popularity enabled Republicans to gain control of Congress, but by 1954 weak Republican leadership enabled Democrats to regain it.

In office Eisenhower largely accepted the modern welfare state bequeathed to him by the New Deal and focused on foreign affairs—negotiating a truce in Korea, and confronting crises in the Middle East, Asia, and Latin America. In a booming economy, he remained a fiscal conservative, but he expanded Social Security benefits and launched an enormous federal program to build new waterways and the interstate highway system. When the Soviet Union launched the world's first space satellite, *Sputnik*, the president came out strongly for federal aid to public education, a decisive turning point in education policy. Faced with a powerful conservative wing in his own party, Eisenhower behind the scenes supported a Senate measure to censure Senator McCarthy, shown opposite, in November 1954 after the Wisconsin Congressman charged top brass in the U.S. Army of harboring communists in the military. The Supreme Court, under Eisenhower appointee Chief Justice Earl Warren, issued its ruling in *Brown v. Board of Education* (1954). For the first time in the nation's history, racial segregation in public places was ruled unconstitutional.

Eisenhower won reelection in 1956. With Southern Democrats hostile to civil rights, and with Republicans almost universally in favor, Eisenhower took 39 percent of the black vote in 1956. In 1957, Congress passed the Civil Rights Act, the first civil rights legislation since Reconstruction. The bill created the U.S. Civil Rights Commission and a civil rights division in the Justice Department.

8. Senator Joseph McCarthy made a political career out of denouncing communist infiltration in government, gaining widespread news coverage. In 1954 the U.S. Senate voted to censure McCarthy for over-reaching in his prosecution of suspected communists.

At the end of his second term Eisenhower remained popular. As a soldier who had fought in two world wars and a president who led the nation through a series of international crises and the beginnings of the civil rights revolution, he understood the profound changes occurring in postwar America. In his farewell address, he warned of rise of the "military-industrial complex" that had emerged with the Cold War.

In 1960, Democrats nominated the telegenic forty-two-year-old senator John F. Kennedy of Massachusetts. He entered the 1960 election opposed by many liberals, including FDR's widow, Eleanor Roosevelt. In fending off his principal liberal challenger, Senator Hubert Humphrey of Minnesota, in the primaries, Kennedy outspent and out-maneuvered his opponent.

His campaign manager, his brother Bobby, used dirty tricks and spread unfair gossip that Humphrey had been a draft-dodger during World War Two, a sharp contrast to John, a war hero. After winning the nomination, Kennedy astutely selected Lyndon Baines Johnson of Texas, the Senate majority leader, as his running mate.

The Republicans nominated Vice President Nixon. Having traveled the globe on Eisenhower's behalf, Nixon pitted his experience in foreign affairs against the inexperienced Kennedy. Any concerns about that inexperience were dispelled, however, during the first-ever televised presidential debate in which the recently ill Nixon appeared tired and the telegenic Kennedy allayed any fears about his understanding of foreign affairs. Kennedy's campaign gained further momentum when he phoned the wife of jailed civil rights leader Rev. Martin Luther King Jr., who had been arrested in Georgia for demonstrating against racial segregation. Kennedy, a Roman Catholic, reinforced his image as a candidate of all the people by speaking on the need for religious toleration and religious diversity in American society.

The 1960 election proved to be one of the closest in American history. Turnout for this election, with 64.3 percent of eligible voters casting ballots, was the highest in modern history. With more than sixty-eight million votes cast, a difference of only 112,803 gave Kennedy the election. Large cities went Democratic, but charges of voter fraud in Chicago marred the victory. Kennedy carried Catholics, Jews, organized labor, and blacks. Despite Lyndon Johnson's presence on the ticket, Nixon took Virginia, Florida, Tennessee, Kentucky, and Oklahoma. With Johnson on the ticket, Democrats carried Texas and other key southern states that enabled Kennedy to win. His support for black civil rights and his Roman Catholicism alienated many voters in the Protestant and segregated South. Still, he carried the rest of it, except Mississippi and Alabama, whose electors cast their votes for a segregationist Democrat, Senator Harry Byrd of Virginia.

The West went for Nixon. Kennedy had put together an uneasy alliance of Northeastern, urban, and Catholic liberals and conservative southerners. He promised to lead America into the "New Frontier." Congress continued under control of the conservative southern Democratic and Republican coalition.

In early 1961, a failed U.S. invasion at the Bay of Pigs in Cuba nearly ruined Kennedy's presidency. A showdown with the Soviet Union a year later when the Soviets placed missiles in Cuba almost led to nuclear war. His ambitious New Frontier domestic program in education, health, and welfare stalled in Congress. A rising civil rights movement pressured the administration to enact new legislation, but Kennedy could not persuade Congress to act.

The nation's conscience was brutally awakened in Birmingham, Alabama, in April 1963 when local officials broke up a peaceful march against segregation organized by Martin Luther King Jr. Americans watching the events on television were outraged to see police with dogs and fire hoses attacking civil rights demonstrators. Three months later Kennedy spoke to the nation asking, "Are we to say to the world . . . that we have no second-class citizens except Negroes?" He called on Congress to pass legislation integrating schools and banning segregation in public facilities. In August 1963, thousands of civil rights activists marched on Washington. King electrified the crowd by declaring that he had a dream that "all of God's children, black men and white men, Jews and gentiles, Protestants and Catholics will be able to join hands" to proclaim "I'm free at last."

Legislation was continuing to languish in Congress when Kennedy was assassinated in Dallas, Texas, on November 22, 1963. Johnson set out to fulfill the late president's promise by pushing civil rights and other pieces of legislation that were stalled in Congress. Pulling out all stops, Johnson, the first southern president since Wilson, got through the Civil Rights Act of 1964, barring discrimination in employment on the basis of race, color, religion, sex, or national origin. The measure would not have passed the Senate without Republican support.

At the same time Johnson called for a "war on poverty." In addition to more federal funding for primary through higher education, the president initiated job training, work relief, adult education, rural assistance, and loans to minority businesses. All were designed, as he promised, to eliminate poverty in a generation.

Johnson's election to the White House in 1964 was a foregone conclusion, even if Republicans had put up a stronger candidate. They nominated Senator Barry Goldwater of Arizona, a staunch conservative who excited the right of the party that opposed the liberal Eastern wing. Goldwater, who barely won the nomination against Governor Nelson Rockefeller of New York, proved to be an easy target. He had voted against the 1964 Civil Rights Act. He did not help matters when he declared in his nomination speech that "Extremism in the defense of liberty is no vice," thus opening the door to charges of extremism. Johnson trounced the Republican, winning more than 60 percent of the vote and an astounding 486 electoral votes to Goldwater's 52. Goldwater barely carried his own state of Arizona, but won the Deep South. Democrats gained thirty-seven seats in Congress, ensuring that liberals dominated both ends of Pennsylvania Avenue for the first time since 1938.

Given this mandate, Johnson called for the creation of a Great Society and pressed for historic social legislation, including Medicare and Medicaid, providing national health insurance for the elderly and needy. Congress passed legislation for funding federal aid to education programs from kindergarten to graduate school. Programs for urban development, urban transit, and public television were established. Congress liberalized immigration and approved the Voting Rights Act (1965), which provided federal oversight of elections in the South. Johnson promised to eliminate poverty in ten years, rebuild

American cities, educate all Americans, provide meaningful jobs, and improve race relations.

The Great Society programs both responded to and promoted social changes brought about by the civil rights movement. The demand for civil rights and growing racial pride among blacks spilled into other ethnic groups including Mexican Americans, Asians, and Native Americans. More radical liberation movements among these groups sprang up. Black leaders Malcolm X, Stokely Carmichael, and H. Rap Brown turned to revolutionary black nationalism and separatism. The rise of a new feminist movement, led by Betty Friedan and Gloria Steinem, also reflected the emergence of a radical consciousness concerning rights and self-identity. They called for equal rights for women and the right to abortion. In 1969, male homosexuals rioted against abusive police practices at New York's Stonewall bar. These liberation

9. Student marchers at University of California, Berkeley in 1965 demanded free speech after the university tried to ban the distribution of political literature on campus. The next year Republican Ronald Reagan was elected governor, playing on voter backlash to campus protests.

movements challenged the traditional vision of the American "melting pot."

Johnson's Great Society raised high expectations in these groups, while creating a backlash among many middle-class and blue-collar whites in the North and the South. Racial riots in the Watts section of Los Angeles, followed by major riots in Chicago and other cities, accelerated this backlash. The following summer, in 1966, race riots broke out in thirty-eight cities across America. The president's decision to escalate a small counter-insurgency effort in Vietnam into a full-scale war sparked protests on college campuses—like the one at the University of California, Berkeley—that spread into a far-reaching antiwar movement as the Vietnam War intensified and more American soldiers were killed. By 1968, liberals within Johnson's own party broke ranks with him.

When antiwar candidate Senator Eugene McCarthy of Minnesota showed surprising strength in the New Hampshire primary, Robert Kennedy announced he was entering the race. In response to the announcement, Johnson told a surprised nation that he would not seek reelection. The following month, civil rights leader King was assassinated in Memphis, Tennessee. Major rioting occurred in the nation's capital and Chicago. Student antiwar protests turned violent at many of America's most prestigious universities. The legacy of Johnson's Great Society programs of Medicare and Medicaid, federal aid to cities and education, and welfare programs endured, but Johnson's America in 1968 stood as a nation divided.

Nixon made one of the greatest political comebacks in modern history by winning the Republican nomination in 1968. The antiwar insurgency within the Democratic Party failed when Kennedy was assassinated by an anti-Zionist extremist the evening he won the California primary. McCarthy's campaign petered out. When Democrats met in Chicago later that summer, Johnson's hand-selected candidate Vice President Hubert

Humphrey won the nomination. Antiwar protesters in Chicago, brutally suppressed by the police acting under orders from the city's mayor, Richard Daley, severely damaged Humphrey. His initial reluctance to denounce the war alienated liberals in his party. The disarray of the Democratic Party opened the way for a third-party candidate, Governor George Wallace of Alabama, a staunch segregationist Democrat running on the American Independent ticket.

Nixon courted southern whites, working-class white ethnic voters, and the suburban middle class by calling for law and order and reform of the "welfare mess," to stop forced busing, and end the war in Vietnam. The strategy paid off, barely. He won 43.4 percent of the popular vote to Humphrey's 42.7 percent and Wallace's surprising 13.5 percent.

In the White House, Nixon pursued a centrist program that kept his Democratic opposition off balance and alienated the far right of his party. In foreign policy, Nixon subordinated ideology through a pragmatic approach that acknowledged a balance of power in the world. He pursued arms control with the Soviet Union through the Strategic Arms Limitation Treaty (SALT I) and opened relations with mainland China even as he ramped up the war in Vietnam, launching a major invasion of Cambodia in 1970. In domestic policy, Nixon expanded welfare programs, directed block grants to state and local governments, and signed a record volume of environmental legislation, including the Clean Air Act. He created the Environmental Protection Agency (EPA), and he pushed for affirmative action programs tied to government contracts. Faced with an economy beginning to experience high inflation (5 percent in 1970), he imposed wage and price controls and in 1971 took the country off the international gold standard, traditionally supported by conservatives.

In 1972, Democrats moved to the left by nominating the antiwar senator from South Dakota, George McGovern. Rallying young antiwar activists and women, the McGovern campaign won delegate slots at the convention through newly imposed party rules that placed quotas on delegations to ensure full representation of women, ethnic minorities, and community leaders. Nixon undercut McGovern's antiwar message when he announced a truce in Vietnam. The Democrat's hastily thrown-together domestic program of high taxes and expanded government proved an easy target for Nixon, who attacked his opponent as an inept radical. The incumbent swamped both the popular vote, polling over 60 percent, and the Electoral College, 520 to 17.

Nixon's victory seemed certain from the beginning. Nevertheless, leaving nothing to chance, his independent Committee to Reelect the President (CREEP) raised millions of dollars by targeting corporations and executives tied to government contracts. The chairman of CREEP, former attorney general John Mitchell, also approved a "dirty tricks" campaign against Democrats. The extent of these tricks became known when Republican operatives were arrested in July while trying to bug phones in the Democratic National Committee headquarters in the Watergate office complex in Washington. When told of this break-in, Nixon tried to cover up links to the White House.

Congressional investigations after the election, spurred by new revelations coming from *Washington Post* reporters Bob Woodward and Carl Bernstein, revealed the president's involvement in the Watergate cover-up. A separate congressional investigation of corruption while he was governor of Maryland led Vice President Spiro Agnew to resign. Nixon selected Representative Gerald R. Ford of Michigan to replace him. By the summer of 1974, Nixon had lost the confidence of congressional Republicans. On August 9, 1974, he became the first president of the United States to resign.

Any notions of politicians as "men of honor" had become a forgotten memory in American politics. Democrats swept into

Congress in the midterm elections of 1974. Many within the Republican Party openly wondered if their party was going the way of the defunct Whig Party. Both conservatism and New Deal liberalism appeared spent. The nation stood traumatized by a decade of war, racial divisions, a deteriorating economy, and scandal.

Chapter 9
Tumultuous politics continued, 1974–present

Five salient factors shaped the context for post–Cold War politics: the demise of the Soviet Union in the 1990s, booms and busts in the economy, increased polarization within the electorate, the continuation of low voter turnout, and the emergence of grassroots activist organizations not necessarily loyal to any political party. Given the large size of government and the growing importance of television, the presidency gained visibility and preeminence as Congress receded in political significance. Party competition remained intense, with both parties incorporating grassroots activist wings that encouraged leaders to take polarized positions.

The presidencies of Gerald Ford (1974–76) and Jimmy Carter (1977–81) represented a transition in American politics from the Vietnam and Watergate eras. Both presidents projected moderation in office; both presidents confronted opposition from a Democratic-controlled Congress; both presidents faced primary challenges in seeking another term; and both candidates lost reelection, Ford in a close election in 1976 and Carter in a landslide defeat in 1980.

Stepping into the White House after Nixon's resignation, Ford sought to reassure a nation shaken by Vietnam and Watergate. Ford pursued his natural inclination toward centrism, but he found his presidency thwarted by Democrats in Congress. His continuation of Nixon's foreign policy and his moderate domestic program created a vacuum on the right. Conservatives coalesced around Ronald Reagan, a former Hollywood actor who had won election as California governor in 1966. As a minority within a minority party, the New Right interjected new moral and national defense issues into politics. In doing so, they tapped into growing complaints among evangelical Protestants, traditional Catholics, and Mormons about a secular culture that had banned prayer in schools, promoted abortion rights, and challenged traditional family values.

Ford dismissed the threat from his right when Ronald Reagan challenged him for the party nomination in the 1976 primaries. Reagan voiced concerns that the nation was in moral, economic, and military decline. When he seized upon Ford's proposed turnover of the U.S.-controlled Panama Canal to the Panamanians, he began winning Republican primaries. In the end, though, Ford got the nomination, but the bruising primaries damaged him in November.

Democrats turned to an outsider, the former governor of Georgia, Jimmy Carter, after he had winnowed a large field of primary challengers. A professed evangelical Christian, former naval officer, and former Democratic governor of a southern state, he appealed simultaneously as an economic liberal and a social conservative. As it was, Carter narrowly defeated Ford, while Democrats continued to control both houses of Congress. The Carter presidency proved, however, to be a missed opportunity. Republicans appeared to have become a permanent minority in Congress, a pitiful 142 to 292 in the House and 38 to 62 in the Senate. Yet even with a Democratic Congress, Carter proved ineffectual. Any popularity he might have enjoyed negotiating a peace treaty between Israel and Egypt was diminished by high inflation and high unemployment. Many wondered if America was in perpetual decline. In 1978, grassroots conservatives scored major congressional victories, even though Democrats continued to control Congress.

By 1980 Carter had alienated the left in his party, including feminists, antinuclear activists, and social liberals. Senator Edward "Ted" Kennedy of Massachusetts, the brother of John and Bobby, challenged Carter for the nomination. Kennedy's bid failed but left Carter damaged. A takeover of the U.S. embassy in Iran by militant students in which more than fifty Americans were held hostage on November 4, 1979, initially boosted Carter's public approval ratings; as the Iranian crisis continued, however, Americans came to see Carter as incompetent.

After fending off a challenge from George H. W. Bush, a Washington insider, Reagan won the Republican nomination. A principled conservative and a pragmatist, Reagan selected Bush as his running mate. Carter, like others before him, underestimated Reagan's appeal to the voters. On Election Day, Reagan won in one of the largest landslides in American history, beating Carter by 9 percentage points, winning 489 electoral votes to Carter's 49, and taking 44 states. Carter was the first Democratic incumbent president since 1888 to lose a bid for reelection. Reagan swept the South, transforming it into a Republican stronghold. Republicans won the Senate and made gains in the House.

Reagan accomplished much in his two terms in office, although the full extent of the "Reagan Revolution" remains a point of contention. The raising of interest rates by a Federal Reserve Bank intent on wringing inflation out of the economy caused a recession in his first year. Afterward, though, the economy boomed. Pragmatically working with congressional Democrats, the president achieved major reform in Social Security by raising contributions and raising the retirement age. In his second term, he undertook a major overhaul of the tax system. His administration pursued deregulation of industry, a policy begun under Carter.

Reagan did not downsize government, although he argued for it. Budget cuts reduced a few social programs, and a modest policy shift occurred through directing more federal funds to states, but a Democratic-controlled Congress (and public opinion) prevented deeper cuts. In 1982, Reagan accepted higher taxes. His hope to balance the budget by spurring economic growth by means of tax rate reductions (so-called supply-side economics) was dashed by huge increases in defense spending.

Reagan pushed for a massive defense buildup, doubling the size of the Pentagon's annual budget. In 1983 he proposed the Strategic Defense Initiative (SDI), an anti-missile-defense system based in outer space—quickly ridiculed by opponents as "Star Wars." At the same time, his administration pursued a war by proxy against a radical pro-Cuban Sandinista government in Nicaragua—which also drew criticism from leftwing grassroots activists.

Reagan cultivated grassroots activists in his own party, especially evangelical Christians—the Christian Right—led by televangelist Jerry Falwell and his Moral Majority organization, and Pat Robertson, founder of the Christian Coalition and Christian Broadcasting Network. The administration kept in close contact with antiabortion organizations and activists, even though attempts to overturn *Roe v. Wade* (1973), a court decision legalizing abortion, failed.

Democrats at the national level remained divided over strategy and vision. Gains made in the 1982 midterms, including twenty-six seats in the House, reinforced a misperception that the general electorate had shifted to the left. Party liberals remained loyal to former vice president Walter Mondale even as a new breed of Democrats—Governor Bill Clinton of Arkansas and Senator Paul Tsongas of Massachusetts—called for new, less liberal, policies. Mondale won the Democratic nomination in 1984 and called for higher taxes to preserve social programs threatened by Reagan cuts. To add excitement to his campaign,

Mondale selected congresswoman Geraldine Ferraro as his running mate, the first woman selected for a national ticket by a major political party.

Mondale's attacks on Reagan came across as desperate. Reagan's ad campaign focused on "Morning in America" and projected an image of a restored nation. He swept the Electoral College and the popular vote.

His second term followed the pattern of many second-term presidents—squandered opportunities. Reagan did achieve a major legislative victory by working with Democratic congressional leaders to pass the Tax Reform Act of 1986. The act reduced the number of tax brackets, dropped the top marginal rate, raised corporate rates, and removed millions of low-income people from the tax rolls by raising the personal exemption. His greatest achievement came in foreign policy, when he announced substantial nuclear arms reductions with reformed-minded Soviet leader Mikhail Gorbachev in 1987.

These achievements were marred, however, by reports that the Reagan administration had traded arms illegally with Iran to help fund the Contras, anticommunist counter-revolutionaries in Nicaragua. This byzantine arrangement had been developed in the National Security Council by Lieutenant Colonel Oliver North and National Security Advisor John Poindexter. Although the scheme was not traced back directly to Reagan, the scandal placed the president on the defensive. Absorbed with the scandal, the administration failed to secure Senate approval for his Supreme Court nominee Robert Bork, a staunch legal conservative and strict constitutionalist. Attacks on Bork in Senate hearings and the liberal press outraged grassroots conservatives. After Bork's defeat in the Senate, Reagan secured the appointment of Anthony Kennedy to the court. There Kennedy joined the court's first female justice, Sandra Day O'Connor, appointed by Reagan in 1981.

Reagan's popularity spilled over to Republican presidential nominee George H.W. Bush in 1988. Bush sought to reassure the Republican base that he too was a Christian who loathed abortion and loved small government. At the Republican convention, he promised the crowd, "Read my lips—no new taxes." In the general campaign he faced Michael Dukakis, a Massachusetts liberal Democrat who made an easy target for Bush. The campaign took a particularly nasty turn when Republican operatives produced a TV spot that accused Dukakis of having given a prison furlough to a convicted felon, Willie Horton, who subsequently raped a young woman and tortured her and her boyfriend. On election night, Dukakis conceded defeat early when Bush won 53.4 percent of the popular vote and forty states.

Bush was the first candidate since Richard Nixon to win the White House while his party lost seats in Congress. His popularity soared when he launched an invasion to oust Panamanian dictator and drug lord Manuel Noriega in 1989. The next year Bush's popularity reached even greater heights when he drove Iraqi troops out of Kuwait in the First Gulf War. After the war, he signed a new treaty with Soviet leader Mikhail Gorbachev to reduce existing arsenals of ballistic missiles. By the end of the year, the Soviet Union had been dissolved.

Intent on showing that he was a conservative with a heart, Bush backed the Americans with Disabilities Act in 1990, which extended civil rights to the disabled. Faced with a $2.7 trillion national debt left over from Reagan and a budget deficit, Bush accepted the Democratic-controlled Congress's proposal in 1991 to raise taxes and cut spending. By breaking his promise not to raise taxes, he earned the wrath of the Republican right and the general disgust of the public, especially when Congress did not cut spending. His appointment of the conservative black Clarence Thomas to the Supreme Court in 1991 failed to win back conservatives.

In 1992 Bush won his party's nomination after a fierce fight against right-wing columnist Patrick Buchanan, who received 25 percent of all Republican votes cast in the primaries. To appease conservatives, Bush gave Buchanan a prime-time spot at the convention in which Buchanan declared a cultural war and turned off moderate voters.

Democratic primaries were equally fierce, resulting in the nomination of Bill Clinton, an obscure governor from Arkansas who had called for his party to move to the center. He sensed that with Bush having been pushed to the right by Buchanan, Democrats could appeal to moderates. His selection of border state Tennessee politician Senator Albert Gore Jr. as his running mate affirmed Clinton's considerable political skills. He targeted Bush for being out of touch with America. A recession in 1991 imparted a resonance to the focus of the Clinton campaign's catchphrase, "It's the economy, stupid."

The emergence of a third-party candidate, Texas billionaire Ross Perot of the Reform Party, inflicted further damage on Bush. Perot's campaign reinforced attacks on the incumbent administration as corrupt, elitist, and out of touch. When Bush's negative ads attacked Clinton, voters shifted from Clinton to Perot rather than to Bush. Clinton carried 32 states in the most sweeping victory for any Democrat since Lyndon Johnson in 1964, although it was still only a plurality. Clinton won self-described independents and moderates, split the large baby boomer vote, and carried 84 percent of blacks. Single women turned out for Clinton, revealing a gender gap for Republicans. Perot's 19 percent popular vote cut heavily into votes that Bush had won in 1988.

Clinton's presidency reflected his experience as governor of Arkansas. During his governorship, he promoted pushing welfare recipients into the workforce through workfare and retraining programs. Welfare reform became one of his great accomplishments in his second term as president. National welfare reform under Clinton had been preceded also in Wisconsin, under Republican governor Tommy Thompson, thereby showing how states often provided the testing grounds for national agendas. During Clinton's presidency, New York mayor Rudy Giuliani developed a community policing policy, which cut the crime rate dramatically. Other cities copied this concept of policing.

Although Clinton ran as a centrist Democrat, conservatives worried that he was not the moderate he claimed to be. Revelations during his campaign that he had a series of extramarital affairs reinforced their view that he lacked the character expected of a president. Clinton's proposal to lift the ban on gays in the military (quickly withdrawn after Pentagon and public protest) and his proposal to nationalize health care through a program drafted by his wife, Hillary, convinced conservatives that he was a liberal hiding under moderate clothing. After twelve years of Republican presidents, Democrats were just relieved that they had reentered the White House, even if Clinton proclaimed he was a centrist in favor of a balanced budget, welfare reform, and only modest expansion of government.

An exceptionally adept politician, Clinton agreed to a "Don't Ask, Don't Tell" compromise policy for gays in the military. He also retreated on national health insurance once it was clear it was not going to pass Congress. His major success came when he garnered Republican support to push through ratification of the North American Free Trade Agreement (NAFTA) in the fall of 1993, against the wishes of organized labor.

In 1994, Clinton found himself on the political defensive when he became ensnarled in three distinct scandals: a sexual harassment suit, an Arkansas land development deal, and allegations that his wife, Hillary Rodham Clinton, had benefited while in Arkansas from insider commodity trading. Conservatives exploited these scandals in 1994. At the same time, Newt Gingrich of Georgia and other conservatives in the House nationalized their campaign with the "Contract with America," promising, if elected, to enact welfare reform, to balance the budget, and to downsize the regulatory state. Their campaign in the 1994 midterm elections drew support from a well-organized conservative movement and a cadre of right-wing talk-radio hosts such as Rush Limbaugh. The strategy paid off when Republicans captured both the House and the Senate. In this "Republican Revolution," the party picked up fifty-four seats in the House and eight in the Senate. It was the first time in forty years they had a majority in the House. Newt Gingrich became Speaker.

Stunned by the midterms, Clinton moved to the right. At the same time, he skillfully attacked the Republicans' proposed budget as hurting the poor. Clinton's veto of the budget and the Republicans' refusal to compromise caused a government shutdown, but an outraged public blamed the Republicans and forced them to back down. Gingrich had over-played his hand. In August 1996, Clinton signed a major welfare reform bill that barred mothers under eighteen from receiving benefits. This further weakened Republican charges that he was not a centrist.

Riding a crest of popularity against a weak Republican candidate, Senator Robert Dole of Kansas, Clinton was reelected in 1996. He received, however, slightly less than 50 percent of the popular vote. (Ross Perot took 8 percent.) This defeat should have tempered conservatives. It did not. When investigators revealed that President Clinton had "inappropriate" relations with a White House intern—a charge he at first denied—House Republicans proceeded with impeachment charges. The American public, however, sided with Clinton. Americans were willing to forgive Clinton for his sexual transgressions, just as they had forgiven Grover Cleveland and Warren G. Harding earlier. In 1998, Republicans lost four seats in Congress, retaining a bare majority in both houses. Blamed for the defeat, Gingrich announced his resignation as House Speaker. After the election, the Senate voted not to convict the president, but the scandal left Clinton politically damaged. His greatest accomplishments were NAFTA, welfare reform, and balancing the budget, largely due to increased revenues from a booming economy.

Everyone knew that the 2000 presidential election was going to be tight. Few realized how tight until the final tally came in. George W. Bush, Texas governor and son of the former president, won the Republican nomination after brilliantly declaring himself a "compassionate conservative." He understood that his base was conservative, while the public accepted the core of the welfare state. Democrats nominated Vice President Gore, the natural successor to Clinton. A booming economy favored Gore, but he refused to link himself closely to the Clinton administration because of the sex scandal. Instead playing on the strong economy, Gore frightened moderate voters by proposing thirty-nine new spending programs in his acceptance speech. He compounded his problems by fighting with Ralph Nader, who decided that Gore was a phony environmentalist and entered the race himself.

An additional 537 disputed votes in Florida would have given Gore the presidency. After three recounts, the election came down to a legal battle over ballots, resulting finally in a U.S. Supreme Court decision in favor of Bush. Gore won the popular vote 48.4 to 47.8 percent but lost the Electoral College 271 to 266. The narrow margin of victory—and charges that he had stolen the election— damaged Bush from the moment he entered the White House. Democrats also ended up narrowly controlling the Senate. In this awkward political environment, the new president pushed a big tax cut and worked with Senator Ted Kennedy to draft the "No Child Left Behind" act linking federal education monies to educational performance standards.

On September 11, 2001, terrorist attacks on the World Trade Center in New York and the Pentagon changed the political landscape in America and had far-reaching global consequences.

The following month, the United States and Western allies launched an invasion in Afghanistan to overthrow the Taliban Islamic regime, which had harbored Osama bin Laden, architect of the 9/11 attacks. While the regime fell, the allies became bogged down in a war of attrition and installing democracy proved difficult. The initial success in Afghanistan misled the Bush administration into thinking that an invasion of Iraq would lead to a similar quick result. The president's forceful response to 9/11 and his rise in the polls carried over to the midterm elections of 2002, when Republicans regained the Senate. American troops, however, became bogged down in a sectarian war after Iraq's dictator Saddam Hussein was overthrown.

In 2004, Bush won reelection against a weak Democratic candidate, Senator John Kerry of Massachusetts. The liberal Kerry's claim to be a war hero in Vietnam came under withering attack from right-wing activists running negative television spots. Bush sailed easily into a second term, and Republicans increased their control of Congress. They appeared ascendant. Republicans in Congress, however, quickly squandered their modest mandate by pushing through self-serving legislation benefiting home districts. Bush's perceived mishandling of a destructive hurricane in the Gulf of Mexico further hurt his public image. By 2006, Americans had grown war-weary. Democrats retook the House and effective control of the Senate in the midterms, a projection of things to come.

The drafters of the Constitution meeting in Philadelphia could not have imagined that more than two hundred years later Americans would elect a black to the presidency. The election was historic in other ways as well. The Democratic primaries pitted the first woman, Hillary Rodham Clinton, against the first black, Barack Obama, seriously contending for the presidency. Tapping into strong antiwar sentiment, especially among youth, Obama won his party's nomination. Republicans turned to U.S. Senator John McCain, a Vietnam War hero. On the campaign trail, the seventy-year-old, often fumbling McCain set a sharp contrast to the cool, highly articulate Obama. The Obama campaign raised record Wall Street money and outspent McCain two to one, micro-targeting voters. The election set a record for the most expensive in American history. Turnout increased, largely among minority voters.

Whatever chances McCain might have had were dashed in mid-September when the American financial system collapsed. The federal government merged several banks and took control of federally sponsored mortgage lenders, Fannie Mae and Freddie Mac. In the crisis, the Bush administration persuaded Congress to pass the Troubled Assets Relief Program (TARP) that provided $700 billion to bail out troubled financial companies. Obama easily defeated McCain, receiving 365 electoral votes to McCain's 173. Democrats expanded their control of the House and took the Senate. Obama's share of the popular vote—53 percent—was high but not historic. Nonetheless he was the first Democrat to receive more than 50 percent since Lyndon Johnson in 1964. His campaign tapped into war weariness, environmentalism, national health care reform, and high hopes for a postpartisan, postracial country.

Obama entered the White House in the worst financial crisis since the Great Depression. With the support of a Democratic Congress, he undertook a bailout of automobile giants General Motors and Chrysler, passed a $700 billion-plus economic stimulus bill, and enacted a controversial compulsory health insurance plan, the Patient Protection and Affordable Care Act. He gradually drew down American troops in Iraq and Afghanistan. Obama's program won widespread support among Democrats but outraged the grassroots right already angry about TARP and the bailout of Wall Street. These conservatives responded by organizing protests on the local level through Tea Party organizations, which used Revolutionary War images of American patriots dumping taxed British tea into the Boston Harbor in 1773.

The volatility of American politics was evident in the 2010 midterms when Republicans retook the House; they gained a

10. In response to George W. Bush's bailout of the financial industry in 2008 and Barack Obama's Affordable Health Care and Patient Protection Act in 2010, grassroots protesters calling themselves the Tea Party challenged establishment Republicans and Democrats. These protesters played upon the theme of early American revolutionaries.

historic sixty-three seats, giving them a majority of 262 seats. They also gained six seats in the U.S. Senate to hold forty-seven seats. Republicans now had their largest majority in the House since 1946, although Democrats kept control of the Senate. These Republican gains came at the expense of moderate Democrats and moderate Republicans, sharpening ideological polarization in Congress. As a result, Republicans in Congress moved farther to the right, heightening polarization in Washington.

Obama won election in 2008 promising to end political polarization. In his bid for reelection in 2012, he reversed course to undertake a highly partisan attack on his opponent, Mitt Romney, a wealthy financier and former Massachusetts governor. Both parties blamed the other side for polarized politics, but whoever was to blame, there was no doubt that partisan politics remained as tumultuous as ever. Republicans in Congress, especially the House, had become more conservative, while moderate Democrats dwindled in their party caucus. Although the American economy had continued to sputter following the 2008 collapse, Obama convinced voters that things might have been worse if he had not provided leadership in this crisis. He downplayed the historic enactment of the Patient Protection and Affordable Care Act (2010) to warn that Romney represented the return of George W. Bush, whose policies had gotten America into the mess it was in. He rallied his base of urban voters, single women, and ethnic minorities to win a close reelection with 51 percent of the popular vote. He faced languid economic growth, continuation of global financial problems, scandals within the administration, and gridlock in government.

The Founders feared factions and political parties as subversive to a harmonious representative republic. From an historical perspective, factions and parties appear to be an inevitable result of democracy. In the twenty-first century, America, it seemed, was entering into a new era marked by political and financial volatility and international turmoil. Many American voters appeared increasingly disenchanted with both political parties and anxiously awaited new leadership and new solutions in a world far different from the eighteenth-century world of the American founders.

References

Chapter 1: The politics of the Constitution, 1787–89

Alexander Hamilton quotation, "Alexander Hamilton to George Washington, September 30, 1790," http://founders.gov/ Washington/05-06-02-0242.

Lee on ratification, Herbert J. Storing, *The Complete Anti-Federalist*, Volume 1 (Chicago: University of Chicago Press, 1992), 142.

Chapter 2: Contentious people and factious parties in the Early Republic, 1789–1824

Hamilton on political factions, Harold Coffin Syrett, *The Papers of Alexander Hamilton*, Volume 19 (New York: Columbia University Press, 1973), 43.

Chapter 3: The age of Democracy, 1816–44

Jackson at a Democratic Party dinner, Donald B. Coles, *The Presidency of Andrew Jackson* (Lawrence: University Press of Kansas, 1993), 62.

Chapter 4: The politics of slavery: prelude to the Civil War, 1844–60

Republican quotation, William E. Gienapp, *Origins of the Republican Party, 1852–1856* (New York: Oxford University Press, 1988), 375.

Chapter 5: Politics in war and Reconstruction, 1861–76

Sumner quotation, Mark E. Neeley Jr., *The Union Divided: Party Conflict in the Civil War North* (Cambridge, MA: Harvard University Press, 2002), 161.

Chapter 6: Gilded Age frustration and the Progressive response, 1877–1918

Hanna on William Jennings Bryan, H. Wayne Morgan, *William McKinley and His America* (Kent, OH: Kent State University Press, reprint, 2004), 181.

Chapter 7: Affluence, depression, and world war, 1920–45

Politicians mock Coolidge's rise to power, Robert H. Ferrell, *The Presidency of Calvin Coolidge* (Lawrence: University Press of Kansas, 1993), 40.

Chapter 8: Early Cold War politics, 1945–74

King speech in Washington in August 1963, Ed Clayton, *Martin Luther King: The Peaceful Warrior* (New York: Simon & Schuster, 2001), 118.

Further reading

Chapter 1: The politics of the Constitution, 1787–89

Berkin, Carol. *A Brilliant Solution: Inventing the American Constitution*. New York: Mariner Books, 2003.

Cornell, Saul. *The Other Founders: Anti-Federalism and the Dissenting Tradition, 1788–1828*. Chapel Hill: University of North Carolina Press, 1999.

Rakove, Jack N. *Original Meanings: Politics and Ideas of the Making of the Constitution*. New York: Vintage, 1997.

Robertson, David Brian. *The Original Compromise: What the Constitution's Framers Were Really Thinking*. New York: Oxford University Press, 2013.

Waldstreicher, David. *In the Midst of Perpetual Fetes: The Making of American Nationalism, 1776–1820*. Chapel Hill: University of North Carolina Press, 1997.

Chapter 2: Contentious people and factious parties in the Early Republic, 1789–1824

Brookhiser, Richard. *James Madison*. New York: Basic Books, 2011.

Ellis, Richard E. *The Jeffersonian Crisis: Courts and Politics in the Young Republic*. New York: Oxford University Press, 1971.

Freeman, Joanne B. *Affairs of Honor: National Politics in the New Republic*. New Haven, CT: Yale University Press, 2001.

McCoy, Drew R. *The Elusive Republic: Political Economy in Jeffersonian America*. Chapel Hill: University of North Carolina Press, 1980.

Rakove, Jack N. *James Madison and the Creation of the American Republic*. New York: Pearson/Longman, 2007.

Risjord, Norman K. *Jefferson's America, 1760–1815*. Madison, WI: Madison House Publishers, 1991.

Sharp, James Roger. *American Politics in the Early Republic: The New Nation in Crisis*. New Haven, CT: Yale University Press, 1993.

Chapter 3: The age of Democracy, 1816–44

Brooke, John L. *Columbia Rising: Civil Life on the Upper Hudson from the Revolution to the Age of Jackson*. Chapel Hill: University of North Carolina Press, 2013.

Earle, Jonathan H. *Jacksonian Antislavery and the Politics of Free Soil, 1824–1854*. Chapel Hill: University of North Carolina Press, 2003.

Ellis, Richard E. *The Union at Risk: Jacksonian Democracy, States' Rights, and the Nullification Crisis*. New York: Oxford University Press, 1987.

Howe, Daniel Walker. *What Hath God Wrought: The Transformation of America, 1815–1848*. New York: Oxford University Press, 2007.

Leonard, Gerald *The Invention of Party Politics: Federalism, Popular Sovereignty, and Constitutional Development in Jacksonian Illinois*. Chapel Hill: University of North Carolina Press, 2002.

Remini, Robert V. *Andrew Jackson*. New York: Harper Perennial, 1998.

Remini, Robert V. *John Quincy Adams*. New York: Times Books, 2002.

Sellers, Charles. *The Market Revolution: Jacksonian America, 1815–1846*. New York: Oxford University Press, 1994.

Silbey, Joel H. *Martin Van Buren and the Emergence of American Popular Politics*. Lanham, MD: Rowman & Littlefield, 2005.

Varon, Elizabeth R. *We Mean to Be Counted: White Women and Politics in Antebellum Virginia*. Chapel Hill: University of North Carolina Press, 1998.

Wilentz, Sean. *The Rise of American Democracy: Jefferson to Lincoln*. New York: W. W. Norton, 2005.

Chapter 4: The politics of slavery: prelude to the Civil War, 1844–60

Ashworth, John. *The Republic in Crisis, 1848–1861*. New York: Cambridge University Press, 2012.

Childers, Christopher. *The Failure of Popular Sovereignty: Slavery, Manifest Destiny, and the Radicalization of Southern Politics.* Lawrence: University Press of Kansas, 2012.

Gienapp, William E. *The Origins of the Republican Party 1852–1856.* New York: Oxford University Press, 1988.

Greenberg, Amy. *A Wicked War: Polk, Clay, Lincoln, and the 1846 Invasion of Mexico.* New York: Vintage, 2012.

Holt, Michael. *The Fate of Their Country: Politics, Slavery Extension, and the Coming of the Civil War.* New York: Hill and Wang, 2005.

Holt, Michael. *The Rise and Fall of the American Whig Party: Jacksonian Politics and the Onset of the Civil War.* New York: Oxford University Press, 2003.

Lambert, Oscar. *Presidential Politics in the United States, 1841–1844.* Durham, NC: Duke University Press, 1936.

Quitt, Martin H. *Stephen A. Douglas and Antebellum Democracy.* New York: Cambridge University Press, 2012.

Silbey, Joel H. *Party Over Section: The Rough and Ready Presidential Election of 1848.* Lawrence: University Press of Kansas, 2009.

Silbey, Joel H. *Storm Over Texas: The Annexation Controversy and the Road to Civil War.* New York: Oxford University Press, 2007.

Chapter 5: Politics in war and Reconstruction, 1861–76

Downs, Gregory. *Declarations of Dependence: The Long Reconstruction of Popular Politics in the South, 1861–1908.* Chapel Hill: University of North Carolina Press, 2011.

Foner, Eric. *Reconstruction: America's Unfinished Revolution, 1863–1877.* New York: HarperCollins, 1988.

Lane, Charles. *The Day Freedom Died: The Colfax Massacre, the Supreme Court, and the Betrayal of Reconstruction.* New York: Henry Holt, 2008.

Lemann, Nicholas. *Redemption: The Last Battle of the Civil War.* New York: Farrar, Straus and Giroux, 2006.

Neely, Mark E. *The Boundaries of American Political Culture in the Civil War.* Chapel Hill: University of North Carolina Press, 2005.

Richardson, Heather Cox. *The Death of Reconstruction: Race, Labor, and Politics in the Post-Civil War North, 1865–1901.* Cambridge, MA: Harvard University Press, 2001.

Simpson, Brooks. *The Reconstruction Presidents.* Lawrence: University Press of Kansas, 1998.

Vorenberg, Michael. *Final Freedom: The Civil War, the Abolition of Slavery, and the Thirteenth Amendment.* New York: Cambridge University Press, 2001.

Chapter 6: Gilded Age frustration and the Progressive response, 1877–1918

Altschuler, Glenn C., and Stuart M. Blumin. *Rude Republic: Americans and Their Politics in the Nineteenth Century.* Princeton, NJ: Princeton University Press, 2001.

Calhoun, Charles W. *The Bloody Shirt to Full Dinner Pail.* New York: Hill and Wang, 2010.

Hollingsworth, J. Rogers. *The Whirligig of Politics: The Democracy of Cleveland and Bryan.* Chicago: University of Chicago Press, 1969.

Keller, Morton. *America's Three Regimes: A New Political History.* New York: Oxford University Press, 2009.

McGerr, Michael E. *The Decline of Popular Politics: The American North, 1865–1928.* New York: Oxford University Press, 1988.

Summers, Mark W. *Party Games: Getting, Keeping, and Using Power in Gilded Age Politics* Chapel Hill: University of North Carolina Press, 2006.

Williams, R. Hal. *Realigning America: McKinley, Bryan, and the Remarkable Election of 1896.* Lawrence: University Press of Kansas, 2010.

Chapter 7: Affluence, depression, and world war, 1920–45

Allswang, John M. *The New Deal and American Politics: A Study in Political Change.* New York: John Wiley, 1978.

Andersen, Kristi. *After Suffrage: Women in Partisan and Electoral Politics Before the New Deal.* Chicago: University of Chicago Press, 1996.

Blum, John Morton. *V Was for Victory: Politics and American Culture During World War II.* New York: Mariner Books, 1977.

Brinkley, Alan. *The End of Reform: New Deal Liberalism in Recession and War.* New York: Vintage, 1996.

Dunn, Susan. *Roosevelt's Purge: How FDR Fought to Change the Democratic Party.* Cambridge, MA: Harvard University Press, 2012.

Fausold, Martin L. *The Presidency of Herbert C. Hoover.* Lawrence: University Press of Kansas, 1988.

Ferrell, Robert H. *The Presidency of Calvin Coolidge: American Presidency.* Lawrence: University Press of Kansas, 1998.

Jeffries, John W. *Testing the Roosevelt Coalition: Connecticut Society and Politics in the Era of World War II*. Knoxville: University of Tennessee Press, 1979.

Patterson, James T. *Congressional Conservatism and the New Deal: The Growth of the Conservative Coalition in Congress, 1933–1939*. Lexington: University of Kentucky Press, 1967.

Richie, Donald. *Electing FDR: The New Deal Campaign of 1932*. Lawrence: University Press of Kansas, 2007.

Smith, Richard Norton. *The Uncommon Man: The Triumph of Herbert Hoover*. New York: Simon & Schuster, 1987.

Ware, Susan. *Beyond Suffrage: Women in the New Deal*. Cambridge, MA: Harvard University Press 1987.

Winkler, Alan. *Home Front U.S.A.: American during World War II*. Wheeling, IL: Harlan Davidson, 2000.

Chapter 8: Early Cold War politics, 1945–74

Bowen, Michael. *The Roots of Modern Conservatism: Dewey, Taft, and the Battle for the Soul of the Republican Party*. Chapel Hill: University of North Carolina Press, 2011.

Chesler, Lewis, Godfrey Hodgson, and Bruce Page. *American Melodrama: The Presidential Campaign of 1968*. New York: Viking, 1969.

Devine, Thomas W. *Henry Wallace's 1948 Presidential Campaign and the Future of Postwar Liberalism*. Chapel Hill: University of North Carolina Press, 2013.

Diggins, John P. *The Proud Decades: America in War and Peace, 1941–1960*. New York: W. W. Norton, 1989.

Donovan, Robert. *Conflict and Crisis: The Presidency of Harry S Truman, 1945–1948*. Columbia: University of Missouri Press, 1996.

Gitlin, Todd. *The Sixties: Years of Hope, Days of Rage*. New York: Bantam, 1993.

Gould, Lewis. *1968: The Election that Changed America*. Chicago: Ivan R. Dee, 2010.

Hamby, Alonzo. *The Imperial Years*. New York: Longman, 1978.

Hamby, Alonzo. *Man of the People: A Life of Harry S. Truman*. New York: Oxford University Press, 1995.

Karabell, Zachary. *The Last Campaign: How Harry Truman Won the 1948 Election*. New York: Vintage, 2001.

Matusow, Allen. *The Unraveling of America: A History of Liberalism in the 1960s*. Athens: University of Georgia Press, 2009.

Miroff, Bruce. *The Liberals' Moment: The McGovern Insurgency and the Identity Crisis of the Democratic Party*. Lawrence: University Press of Kansas, 2007.

Oshinsky, Michael. *A Conspiracy So Immense: The World of Joe McCarthy*. New York: Easton Press, 1983.

Rorabaugh, W. J. *The Real Making of the President: Kennedy, Nixon, and the 1960 Election*. Lawrence: University Press of Kansas, 2012.

Smith, Richard Norton. *Thomas E. Dewey and His Times*. New York: Simon & Schuster, 1982.

Chapter 9: Tumultuous politics continued, 1974–present

Collins, Robert M. *Transforming America: Politics and Culture During the Reagan Years*. New York: Columbia University Press, 2009.

Courtwright, David T. *No Right Turn: Conservative Politics in a Liberal America*. Cambridge, MA: Harvard University Press, 2010.

Critchlow, Donald T. *The Conservative Ascendancy: How the Republican Right Rose to Power in Modern America*. Lawrence: University Press of Kansas, 2011.

Hayward, Steven F. *The Age of Reagan: The Fall of the Old Liberal Order, 1964–1980*. Roseville, CA: Prima Publishing, 2001.

Wilentz, Sean. *The Age of Reagan: A History, 1974–2008*. New York: Harper, 2003.

Index

Index

Index